Leaders Lead
The mindset and skillset of
real-life leadership.

Jeffrey J. DeWolf

W0009172

Copyright © 2019 Jeffrey J. DeWolf

All rights reserved.

ISBN: 9781690037897

DEDICATION

To leaders who really lead and those who aspire to start today.

CONTENTS

ACKNOWLEDGMENTS

I want to recognize the part my wife, Deb, has played in my development as a leader and a *human*. Her steadfast persistence in pushing me to grow and change is the only reason I would even dare to write about leadership. I'm grateful for, and amazed by, her capacity to endure nearly three decades with a husband/leader characterized more by good intentions than real-life actions. If she had allowed me to continue in my lazy pseudo-leadership, I shudder to think about who I would be today.

In addition, I want to both thank and *apologize* to my precious children, Lydia, Caleb, Hannah, and Chloe for putting up with me as their family leader. I look back and can't help but have regrets about my efforts (or lack thereof) to be an intentional, servant-leader dad. My prayer is that you'll recognize the good, learn from the not-so-good, and allow me the chance to share what I've learned as you lead your own lives and families.

Finally, I want to also recognize the efforts of my eldest daughter, Lydia, as editor of this book. She not only perfected the grammar and formatting so my thoughts could be communicated properly, but her keen eye for content and communication clarity was also immensely helpful.

LEADERS LEAD

INTRODUCTION

There are books written every day by *experts*. These authors are typically great role-models, highly esteemed, and experienced in the subject matter about which they write.

Countless leadership books are produced by great leaders of people, like high-ranking military commanders, retired CEOs, former politicians, and celebrated management consulting gurus.

The book you're holding is different. It was written by someone who, while moderately successful at climbing the leadership ladder, didn't figure out what leading really was until much later.

I always claimed to have "leadership skills." In fact, I listed *Leadership Skills* on the little bullet-point list of other qualifications at the bottom of my resume even as I graduated from college in 1989.

What a joke.

As I look back on various job interviews, part of me wishes an astute interviewer had said, "Hmm, I see leadership skills are listed here. Tell me what that means…"

I likely would have gulped and then performed a tap-dance routine that would make Ben Vereen proud.

In those days, and well into my career in corporate America, I had no idea what leadership really was. I, like many, was distracted by the stereotypical, unconscious bias-driven image of leadership: Charisma. Extroversion. Effective verbal communication. Persuasiveness. Energy. Greying temples, and a 6'3" physical presence.

That was me.

It wasn't until much later and after a couple of ego-shattering gut-punches that I began to understand what differentiates real leaders from those who just occupy a box on an organizational chart: Action.

Action and real-life behaviors performed every day turn a person from someone with a *title* into someone with a *following*.

FOUR TYPES OF LEADERS

I think there are four types of leaders in the world. The first type I call the *Unaware*. These leaders don't even know what they don't know. They lack practical leadership skills and self-awareness. They don't know what they should or shouldn't be doing in their role as a leader of people. Often, this knowledge gap is innocent, and they have never received training, coaching, or encouragement regarding the requirements of leadership.

The second type of leader I call the *Aware But Don't Care*. These leaders know what's expected of them and what their people need, but don't really care. It's all about them and their career. They enjoy being served as the boss and bask in their power and position.

The third type of leader are those I call the *Aware With Good Intentions*. These are typically good people who know what's needed and expected of them but just never get around to doing anything. They're the ones that will say, "I know I should be meeting with my people, but I'm just so stinkin' busy." This may be the most insidious type of leader. You can train and coach the *Unaware* leader. You can discipline and even replace the *Aware But Don't Care* leader, but it's more difficult to deal with the genuinely nice, hard-working leader who can't seem to get around to doing important things. However, when it comes to people getting what they need from their leader, this type is just as bad as the first two.

The fourth type of leader is the one that I call *Aware With Action*. These are the leaders who put their conviction about leading into action and demonstrate behaviors every day as needed. When a person is this type of leader, people follow. People have what they need to do their jobs and enjoy work: information, communication, feedback, guidance, coaching, correction, development, appropriate autonomy, and relationship.

For most of my career, I would put myself in the category of *Unaware*. I wasn't specifically resisting the demands of leadership, but I was largely naïve about what leading people really meant. As I got older, I would say I became more of an *Aware With Good Intentions* type. I believed in the importance of leadership behaviors, but I just never got around to doing them. I allowed *my* interests, aspirations, and personal goals to drive how I spent my time. I would focus my energies on what *I* was interested in, and would avoid the things that I found boring, unfamiliar, uncomfortable, or difficult. Maybe this sounds like you, too. If it does, you are not alone. It is exhausting to do things we don't feel like doing. It stretches us out of the comfort zones in which we've lived and led our whole lives.

I'm excited to say that I have seen some personal growth over the last several years in this area. It's still very difficult for me to prioritize the necessary tasks of leadership when I'm busy in creative mode, sales mode, or focused on future opportunities. I still tend to avoid the things that require more intentional effort on my part. However, as I often tell leaders who struggle in the same way, it gets easier with practice. As we prioritize the things of leadership, and stretch out of our natural comfort zones, we build elasticity into our personality and leadership style.

While many things will still require a stretch, the energy it takes to do them lessens over time as we retrain our brains to do the things that don't come naturally.

THE ORIGIN OF REAL-LIFE LEADERSHIP

A few years ago, my business was at a crossroads. I had spent several years doing culture assessments and employee surveys for clients that uncovered practical issues affecting employee job happiness, engagement, satisfaction, and loyalty. I began to see an obvious trend in the data. I saw the vast majority of employee dissatisfaction being driven by one key thing: *Leadership*. Most of the pain points identified in our survey processes could be clearly tied to things leaders were doing, or things leaders were *not* doing. Some of the issues were in the domain of executive leadership, but many were tied to an employee's direct supervisor or department manager. It became painfully obvious to me that for companies to improve their levels of employee satisfaction and loyalty, they needed to invest in developing leaders. They desperately needed to teach them what it means to really lead, and then expect them to do it.

I often say that if you gave me $10,000 to spend on "employee engagement," I'd spend $9,900 on teaching leaders to really lead, and $100 on a pizza party.

The contents of this book, and the associated training program called Real-Life Leadership™ offered by Wolf Prairie and its network of independent facilitator-coach partners, are the result of data collected in our employee survey efforts, personal observations as a corporate guy and consultant, and the obvious influence of the great leadership teachers of our time.

While the table of contents in this book doesn't represent an *exhaustive* list of leadership behaviors and actions, it is a very good place to start. As we move through the chapters, we start by investigating the distinction between "leadership" and "management," do a bit of self-assessment, and then move into the tangible actions and behaviors required of leaders at all levels.

It is easy to look at this as a leadership *to-do* list. I'm not ashamed to be tipping scales toward leadership to-dos, behaviors, and actions. Based on my experience, many of us would benefit from *doing* more. However, another key message flows through each of the following chapters: the true leader's heart and the proper leadership mindset. Leadership not only has a *to-do* list, but it also has an important *to-be* list. Without a proper mindset characterized by humility, devotion, integrity, servant-orientation, and a commitment to being the kind of person others want to follow, your to-do list will fall short of making you the kind of leader your team needs.

In each chapter, I will attempt to communicate why the issue is so important. It is my goal to first speak to your heart, so that you will understand what's at stake as you work through the content in each chapter.

THREE POINTS, FIVE QUESTIONS, AND ONE ACTION

It's my primary objective to provide you with simple strategies and methods that you'll be able to apply to your daily personal and work lives immediately.

Research[1] shows that if we don't review and apply what we learn right away, we will quickly lose up to 90% of that new knowledge.

What a colossal waste of time.

---

[1] *Replication and Analysis of Ebbinghaus' Forgetting Curve*, Jaap M. J. Murre and Joeri Dros, 2015.

So, to help make this short book a resource for continued change and real-life application, each chapter will conclude with *three main points to review*, *five questions to consider* for personal reflection, and *one action to take* so the information can be applied immediately. Thank you for joining me on this journey. I'm excited to act not as your guru or role-model, but as your imperfect guide and friend.

I claim only to be one beggar showing other beggars where to find food. The information that follows in this small volume represents the daily bread of leadership. While not intended as *all* that leadership represents, it contains much of the basic nutrition needed to effectively lead people every day.

1 THE LEADERSHIP/MANAGEMENT DISTINCTION

The first question is whether there really *is* a leadership/management distinction. Writers love to come up with pithy little statements to differentiate between these two terms. You know the type: "Management is getting people to do things, leadership is getting them to want to do them." Or the one by one of my leadership heroes, Peter Drucker, that says, "Management is doing things right, leadership is doing the right things." People love to try to distinguish management from leadership by placing leadership on some sort of pedestal. It's as if they are saying that leadership is a higher order skill than management.

I think that this is a false dichotomy, and I have a very different view. Rather than seeing some sort of hierarchy that starts with *supervisor,* then moves to *manager,* then finally to *leader,* I see people as either leaders or not leaders. Practically speaking, at work, one is either an individual contributor or a leader. I don't care whether you lead three people pushing brooms or are the CEO of a Fortune 500 company, you are a leader and as such you have special responsibilities for the people under your care. This applies to formal supervision and to those that lead project teams without direct supervision, but nevertheless are responsible for the results of that team.

I will say that I do make one additional concession about this. There is truth to the idea that even if no one formally reports to you, you are still a leader. If you are a parent, an older sibling, or a coach, then you are a leader in your personal life. Even if you are none of those things and are truly alone, you are still the leader of your own life. When we talk about people, we might remark, "Look at the kind of life he *leads*!" At a person's death, one might say, "She *led* a good life." If nothing else, you are leading the life your future self will have. Who you are now and the actions you take now will affect the life that your future self will experience.

I hope you don't see leadership as something to focus on after you've achieved some certain level of organizational success. Leadership is about *now*, and it's about everyone. This book is for anyone who acts as a leader of people or aspires to formally manage people in the future. I hope that you will focus more on what leadership is and how it plays out in real life, and less on drawing a distinction between managing and leading, because really, they go together.

Leading without management is not leading. It's wandering aimlessly, hoping people will follow. On the other hand, effective management requires leadership. One definition of management is *the process of dealing with or controlling things or people.* By that definition, you can see that a narrow focus on management as just trying to control people is a terrible way to lead. Who would ever describe their favorite boss as someone who did a really good job of "dealing with and controlling" them?

Rather than distinguish a person as a *manager* versus a *leader*, I would simply make the distinction between being a good leader and a bad one. A good leader leads fully, with that leadership taking on many forms, behaviors, and actions. A bad leader is more one-sided, focused on a couple of elements of leadership, while ignoring many of the others.

In short, it might help to think of the management/leadership distinction this way: *Leading well requires, among other things, management. Managing well requires all aspects of leadership.*

WHO YOU ARE OR WHAT YOU DO?

Another debate that I want to address before we dive into the content of this book is whether leadership is *who you are* or *what you do*. It has become fashionable to emphasize that leadership is not a list of things to do. People love to focus on more esoteric and philosophical elements of leadership rather than a bunch of behaviors and tasks that make up a leader's day. It's as if to say that a focus on leadership to-dos is just too pedestrian for advanced leadership scholars such as ourselves...

However, I think it is important to emphasize here that when it comes to this argument, leadership is a *both/and* proposition not an *either/or*. You can't have leadership without tangible, practical action taking place every day. Real-life leadership is measurable by the things we do for our people week in and week out.

On the other hand, I will also say that you won't have tangible practical action taking place every day if you don't have the internal character required of leadership. So, while it may sound like a cop-out, leadership is both who you are and what you do.

I will share a solid list of leadership to-dos throughout this book, but those actions and behaviors will only occur after you embrace the *need* for them. Without having the heart of a leader who cares deeply for your team and the mission of your organization, it will be extremely difficult to be consistent in the behaviors and tasks of leading.

I often say that leadership is not for everyone. Many times, I have asked people if they really want to be in leadership, or just want a larger paycheck. I have found that most people want more money, and the only way they know to get it is to be promoted to supervisor or manager. Then once in that job, they enjoy the paycheck but lack the discipline and fortitude to do the tasks of leadership.

A person who desires to be in a supervisory role needs to count the cost. Leadership is not the perks. It is not a title and a larger office. It is a burden. It's a responsibility that comes with demands on your time and attention. It requires both a heart for people and a commitment that plays out in real-life observable behaviors.

As you move through the rest of this book, I hope you do so with the understanding that while it addresses practical real-life leadership tasks like planning, delegating, coaching, addressing conflict, and more, those things originate in character. They flow from the heart of a person who cares.

THREE POINTS, FIVE QUESTIONS, AND ONE ACTION

Three Points to Review

- The distinction is not between *leadership* and *management*, it's between *good* leadership and *bad* leadership.

- Leading well requires good management practices, and managing well requires a fully committed leader.

- Who you are is just as important as what you do, because from your leadership heart will flow your leadership actions.

Five Questions to Ask

1. Do I subconsciously think that "leading" is for those in higher-level positions than my own?

2. Do I recognize that I'm a leader even in my personal life and family, and as such, people are depending on me?

3. Is my basic view of leading that I'm the boss and others are here to serve my purposes?

4. Do I spend most of my time thinking about *my* own needs, career or future?

5. What leadership behaviors are flowing out of my heart in my situation today?

One Action to Take

✓ Choose one person who you know will be honest with you and ask this question: "What five descriptive words would you use to describe my leadership style?"

2 OMNI-DIMENSIONAL LEADERSHIP

Leadership is one of the most written about and talked about topics in the world. It's been that way for decades. Every day, new books are published, interviews are conducted, and keynote speeches are delivered about this thing called leadership.

Why is that?

I think it's because of two reasons. First, it's because when leaders actually lead, it changes *everything*. There is nothing more important in organizations, or impactful to culture and results, or necessary for happy, productive employees. On the flipside, bad or missing leadership also impacts everything…for the worse.

The second reason we keep talking about leadership is because writers, researchers, and speakers are still trying to break through the noise and get leaders to really change and lead.

In my experience helping organizations with culture, employee satisfaction, and engagement issues, I've seen the devastating effects of bad, negligent, and ineffective leadership. And I'm not just pointing the finger at top executives, I'm talking about supervisors, managers, and leaders at every level. From the first line to the "C-Suite," everyone who manages even one other person plays a critical role in the success of those people and, ultimately, the organization.

If the people in these leadership roles have such an impact on the success of the organization, it's not surprising that we care about helping leaders improve. But despite all the noise and the workshops and the professional development programs, we still find ineffective leadership at play in our organizations.

Why is there such a disconnect between intention and performance?

I believe the main reason so many leadership training programs fail is that they focus too much on leadership skills and not enough on leadership commitment. Said another way, they focus on skillset, but not mindset.

It was Yogi Berra who said, "Baseball is ninety percent mental...and the other half is physical." To borrow from Yogi, I think growth toward becoming an effective leader is ninety percent mindset...and the other half is skillset.

You may have noticed that much has been said recently about "servant" leadership, humility, and emotional intelligence in leaders. These concepts are resonating with many because they're loaded with truth and have a heavy focus on a proper mindset. We'll explore the concept of a proper mindset more in-depth later on, but first, let's see why these concepts are effective in practice.

Start by breaking leadership down to its most basic purpose. It's about getting results done through people, right? But results only happen when people are successful doing the jobs assigned to them.

In other words, leaders are only successful when their people are successful. And people are only successful when they have what they need to do their jobs well. Therefore, the main job of the leader is to meet employees' basic needs, protect them, guide them, develop them, and ensure they're productive.

The servant leadership concept and others like it are powerful. It's powerful and moving and motivating when leaders adopt the right mindset, humble themselves, and put the needs of their people above their own.

A LESSON FROM HISTORY

One day during the American war for independence, George Washington rode up to a group of soldiers trying to raise a beam to a high position. The corporal overseeing the work kept shouting words of encouragement, but they couldn't manage to do it.

After watching their lack of success, Washington asked the corporal why he didn't join in and help. The corporal replied quickly, "Do you realize that I am the corporal?" Washington very politely replied, "I beg your pardon, Mr. Corporal, I did."

Washington then dismounted his horse and went to work with the soldiers until the beam was put into place. Wiping the sweat from his face, he said, "If you should need help again, call on Washington, your commander in chief, and I will come."[2]

George Washington was known for many great qualities. One was his reticence to seek and hold positions of leadership. In nearly every case, he had to be convinced, and sometimes cajoled, to assume power. There was even an effort to crown Washington as a king of sorts, an effort that he quickly rejected. What a refreshing contrast that is to the literal campaigning for leadership positions for personal gain so prevalent in leaders of today.

Washington was counting the cost of leadership. He understood the requirements and sacrifices it would take to fully assume the role of leader. When he finally agreed to lead, he did it with a rare balance of vision, courage, skill, devotion, and, perhaps most importantly, humility.

It's important to note that humility and relationship-focus does not mean weak and soft. There are times when toughness, courage, and energy are very necessary. For people to enjoy their jobs and thrive, they need to see that their leaders are both competent *and* caring. This phenomenon can be hard to find, but it is a potent combination. When people feel cared for by a strong, competent, and compassionate leader, they relax and experience a sense of peace and trust. They may even, dare I say, enjoy being at work.

The dual nature of competence-plus-compassion, strength-plus-humility, or skill-plus-character in leadership demonstrates an important concept: True leadership requires us to embrace a mindset that prioritizes a multi-dimensional set of skills and behaviors.

---

[2] From *The 5 Levels of Leadership*, by John C. Maxwell.

DIFFERENT "DIMENSIONS" OF LEADERSHIP

I have long been enthralled with personality theory. Early in my adolescent years, someone showed me the *Myers-Briggs Type Indicator (MBTI)* and its abbreviated cousin, the *Keirsey Temperament Sorter.* I remember being captivated by the descriptions of the various types and how accurately they described my tendencies and those of my friends. I think I've always loved personality assessments because of the comfort I took from them. When I see myself in research-backed, validated descriptions, I feel a sense of belonging. I feel less like a freak of nature, and more like one of a group of other "freaks" trying to cope with natural instincts and behavior patterns.

Later in life, I discovered the DISC assessment, developed by William Moulton Marston in 1940. It is an excellent, easy-to-apply tool which (unfortunately for his descendants) was never copyrighted by Marston.

One of my first experiences with a DISC-based assessment was found in a book called *The 8 Dimensions of Leadership* by Sugerman, Scullard, and Wilhelm. It was this book that first connected personality type with leadership for me. I loved it.

Once a series of questions is answered, the assessment identifies the assessment-taker as having one of eight primary "dimensions" of leadership. The dimensions are displayed on a circle divided into eight "pie" slices. (See Figure 1.0)

1. Pioneering
2. Energizing

3. Affirming
4. Inclusive
5. Humble
6. Deliberate
7. Resolute
8. Commanding

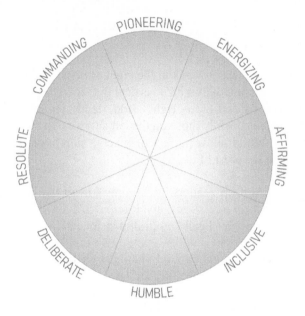

Figure 1.0

The authors explain that each of us enjoys a primary leadership dimension driven by our personality type, experiences, and sometimes our role models. However, effective leadership requires an awareness of and commitment to developing ourselves in the behaviors of all eight dimensions.

The dimensions furthest from our primary dimension typically take the most energy and effort for us to embrace. The good news is that with practice and discipline, we become more comfortable with the skills and behaviors found "across the circle."

When we lead, different circumstances call for different leadership dimensions or priorities. Sometimes we need to be commanding, pioneering, or energizing. At other times, we need to be more affirming, inclusive, or humble. At still other times, we need to be more deliberate and resolute.

A simple way to look at the eight dimensions circle is by dividing it in half with a vertical line down the middle. Dimensions on the right side tend to prioritize relationships, while those on the left side tend to prioritize results. While not a perfect or precise summary, this is accurate for most of us.

To sum it up, leadership requires a heart that's set on both results *and* relationships. It requires that we be well-rounded, or what I call "omni-dimensional."

Though this may sound simple, sometimes even our own natures can get in the way. As I've studied personality types over the years and the impact they have on how we think and act, one thing is clear: Our personality type, as shaped by both our genetics and our experiences, strongly influences how we relate to others, and therefore how we tend to lead.

We as leaders, even more than others, need to explore our own tendencies and be honest about what we find. We're all wired to feel most comfortable with a few dimensions of leadership, but not all of them.

Let's be honest, there are some aspects of leading that we like, and some that we don't. It's human nature to do the things we like and avoid the things we don't, but leadership is not simply being one-dimensional and ignoring the things that are hard, uncomfortable, or awkward.

True leadership happens when we tackle the aspects of leading that we don't feel like doing. Let me say that another way: We are truly leading when we *do* the things we don't feel like doing. "Lead" is an action verb. "Leading" is made up of behaviors and actions that we *do* because we know they're important and our people need them. We lead when we acknowledge our limitations, but understand that it's necessary to do things that we dislike or that make us uncomfortable.

The good news is that we *can* grow our skills as we intentionally stretch out of comfort zones and practice the behaviors that don't come naturally to us. In fact, with practice, we can even grow our comfort zones themselves.

If you manage people, regardless of your level or the size of your staff, you've been entrusted with the most valuable resource of your organization: its people. Let's be good stewards of those resources and commit to growing in all dimensions of leadership.

THREE POINTS, FIVE QUESTIONS, AND ONE ACTION

Three Points to Review

- There is often a disconnect between being in leadership positions and doing the things of leadership.

- Leaders are human and will therefore resist and

avoid things that are unpleasant or make them uncomfortable.

- Leaders truly lead when they become intentional, stretch out of natural dimensions (comfort zones), and become omni-dimensional by engaging in all the behaviors required of effective leaders.

Five Questions to Consider

1. Do I see myself as someone to be served by the people on my team, or as a servant of my team?

2. Do I show my team that I'm with them, working for their best interests and that of the organization?

3. What have I done the past week that made me stretch out of my comfort zone?

4. When I look at the common skills and behaviors around the 8-Dimensions circle, which do I need to improve immediately?

5. Am I practicing the things that don't come naturally to me?

One Action to Take

✓ Go to your current team, tell them you want to get better as a leader, and ask them to identify one thing you should start doing more of that would help them be more successful or comfortable in their jobs.

3 OWNING TIME

Imagine if every morning someone deposited $86,400 into your checking account.

It is money provided with no strings attached. You can spend it, invest it, or give it away, it's up to you. However, every night, whatever is not withdrawn by you is removed. It vanishes from your account. The next morning, a fresh $86,400 is deposited. What would you do?

Wouldn't you be careful every day to think about what to do with that money? Seriously. How often would you forget to withdraw it?

Probably not very often.

I'm guessing that deciding what to do with that free money would be one of the first things on your list. You'd withdraw it and spend it, or at least transfer it into your IRA or 401k account. Maybe you'd buy some hot stocks or write a large check to your church or favorite charity. Maybe you'd withdraw a few stacks of hundreds and drive downtown to hand them out to those in need. The point is, you wouldn't just let it slip away or waste it.

So, why this crazy illustration?

Every day, each of us is given 86,400 seconds of precious time. It's ours to spend, invest wisely, or give away. Every night, whatever is not used is gone. There's no carrying it over to the next day. It's gone.

Taking ownership of our available time is important for everyone, but it is *critical* for leaders of people. Leaders have a special responsibility—a responsibility to do the important tasks of leadership. And tasks take time. Tasks literally *take* real minutes and hours from our day, just as someone would take money out of our bank account.

If our days become too full of ineffective meetings, distractions, and non-priority activities, we tend to ignore our role as a leader. We move from crisis to crisis, fighting fires, multi-tasking, and generally exhausting ourselves until there's no time or willpower left to actually do the things of leadership. Contributing to this is the fact that usually our own bosses don't specifically hold us accountable to perform the tasks of leadership. They too are focused on their own urgent projects and obtaining from us the tangible performance results expected.

Think about it. When was the last time your boss pulled you aside and said, "I'm giving you a lower performance rating because the amount of coaching you did for your people was inadequate this year"?

Before we can learn to apply even the most basic daily leadership and management techniques, we need to really understand the value of time. We need to learn to protect it, maximize it, and really start to "own" it.

Owning time is not simply *managing* time. Owning time reflects an attitude toward time that goes beyond being efficient and controlling it. When we own our time, we start to see it as the most valuable, non-renewable resource in the universe. We protect it. We reserve it and preserve it for the most important things.

FOCUS

In the HBO documentary *Becoming Warren Buffett*, there's a scene where Buffett and his friend Bill Gates attended an event together. The host asked those in attendance to write down the one thing that they each felt contributed most to their success.

Buffett and Gates wrote down the same word on their respective papers: *Focus*.

Focus is often regarded as paying attention to the things that matter most, but it also means focusing on one thing at a time.

Research continues to pour in about the dangers of multi-tasking.[3] Brain science is showing us that frequent interruptions, jumping from task to task, and attempting to juggle diverse activities and projects restricts productivity and quality of work. Instead, it's better for us, and more productive, to structure our time expenditures, reduce distractions, and attempt to focus (whenever possible) on one thing at a time.

---

[3] *Integrating knowledge of multitasking and interruptions across different perspectives and research methods*, by Janssen, Gould, Li, Brumby, and Cox, 2015.

To continue the time-money comparison with which we started this chapter, owning our time is very similar to the discipline of financial budgeting. Why do we take time to set up a budget and monitor our expenditures against that budget? It's to ensure that we spend our money on the things that are most important: the things that align with our vision, support our strategy, and accomplish our goals.

While I'm admittedly not very disciplined about budgeting in real life, I do understand its importance. Without at least some budget constraints, we run the risk of spending our funds on less important or frivolous things. It's not good to run out of the year's money in October.

So, back to the real world of daily life. How do we practically and tangibly start to take more ownership over our time to ensure it is spent on the most important things? Here are three practical ideas to consider.

First, turn off most of the notifications on your phone. No more Pavlovian responses to the "ding." The marketing email from Walmart can wait. The notification that your Amazon purchase has shipped can wait. And dare I say, even the text message from your mom...can usually wait.

Mobile application developers want nothing more than to have your eyeballs glued to their app as often as physically possible. In many cases, their ad revenue depends on it. So, for love all that is holy, deactivate notifications for all ten of your social media accounts. Seeing that little icon on your screen gives you one more thing to process off your to-do list. Don't fall victim to the mental manipulation of the mobile app marketers! They are stealing your valuable time.

Second, block off specific times in your day to read and answer emails. If you still get something called voicemails, do the same with those. (If you don't know what those are, Google it or ask someone born before 1985.) Avoid the temptation to look up from what you are doing to read and answer every time an email drops into your inbox. This is really hard. For me, getting that email feels like someone just dropped something new on to my to-do list without permission. I get the urge to see what it says. What if it's that signed customer contract I've been waiting for? What if it's an important request from a client or team member? So I peek. I stop the thing I'm working on or thinking about and flip over to my email screen. Then, a new battle ensues. After I check, do I go back to the thing I was doing, or just deal with the email right then and there? My mind starts evaluating the trade-off. Should I invest the few minutes to respond and *get it off my to-do list,* or do I stay focused on the important project I'm working on right now? We usually underestimate the time it takes to get our original train of thought back onto the tracks. Avoid the entire derailing debate by planning specific times to deal with emails, instead of succumbing to the constant distraction and second-guessing.

Third, consider using a focusing strategy like the Pomodoro technique to give structure to a specific project or effort needing focused concentration. Named after the tomato-shaped kitchen timer, a Pomodoro is a 25-minute interval of focused, uninterrupted work on a specific task, followed by a five-minute break from that task. After four of these cycles, a longer 15-minute break is recommended. During the short and longer breaks, it is important to stand up, stretch, and move around a bit. That's the time to check a text message, answer a *quick* email or chat with a coworker. The Pomodoro technique is an interesting and research-supported productivity tool.

You can use a real kitchen timer or download a simple app to replicate the ticking and classic metallic *riiiiinnnng* of that little plastic classic.

In fact, even as I work on this chapter, I'm using the Pomodoro technique to stay focused on writing this book. Believe me, in the time it has taken to write the last several paragraphs, I've had to ignore several micro-demands for my attention.

Focus is even more of a challenge for those working in open office environments. In these cases, I highly recommend that you adopt a strategy that allows you to work without interruption for at least a portion of your day. One of my clients created bright red laminated cards that they placed in their workstation to indicate they were engaged in a Pomodoro. It provided a visual, unspoken reminder to coworkers that an interruption (unless an emergency) needed to wait for at least 25 minutes.

Whether you embrace the specific Pomodoro technique or not, the principle of focused effort followed by a short break is a sound strategy. Find a method that works for you. You won't regret it.

PRIORITIZATION

Since our time is limited, prioritizing what we spend it on is critical. There are always more demands for our time and attention than there are hours in the day. Wise leaders carefully evaluate where to spend their time.

Ironically, this only happens by prioritizing the act of prioritization.

By nature, I'm not given to planning and prioritization.

My personal style is more to wing it. I have a hard time investing effort in planning, forecasting, and preparing. Something deep inside me wants to get moving and start making progress, so sitting around planning and prioritizing can feel like inertia to me. Essentially, my instinct is to just jump in, let things unfold, and hope I get everything done. While hope and optimism are wonderful and needed, I think we can all agree that hope is not an effective or wise *strategy*.

Since *my* first internal battle is even pausing to think through my priorities, I have to force myself to make time to plan. I will often skip high level prioritization and lower level to-do list planning. Maybe you struggle with this as well. Or maybe you are one to faithfully create to-do lists, but you don't evaluate that list in light of priorities.

This doesn't need to be an extensive or exhaustive process. Maybe it's a few minutes at the beginning of the day or the week to assess priorities and plan specific tasks. Maybe it's at the end of a workday to organize your thoughts and plans for the coming morning.

To bring this idea of prioritization into the real world, here are a few simple strategies that will help you get the right things done.

First, tackle the hard tasks when you're freshest. For most, this is earlier in the day. For some, it might be a little later, after a couple cups (or pots) of coffee. As the hours of our day drag on, our energy levels tend to fade. Hard tasks are those that require the most thought, problem solving, and mental energy. These are the things you see on your list and then say, "I don't have the time or capacity to tackle *that* right now." In short, don't save the tasks requiring the most brain power for the end of the day when your energy is low. When you knock the hard stuff off your list early, you'll feel like you're coasting downhill the rest of the workday.

Second, get the most unpleasant thing done first. This is similar to the point I just made. Unpleasant things are hard to do. Often, things that push us out of our comfort zones feel very unpleasant, uncomfortable, and awkward.

Mark Twain once said, "Eat a live frog the first thing in the morning, and nothing worse will happen to you the rest of the day." So, when you get to work in the morning, eat that frog! You'll be shocked at the relief you feel having that unpleasant task behind you.

Third, identify a "top three to-do list." I realize that we always have more than three things on our to-do list, but each day, make your list and circle the three things that are most important to move you toward your goals. Factor in the difficulty, time-urgency, and what's at stake for you. If you have a couple things that, if not accomplished, will have a significant negative impact on you, circle them. If you can end the day having completed your three most important tasks, it will have been a very effective day. Remember, the tasks of supervising, coaching, and management should be on those lists, too. We'll explore more about that idea later.

MEETINGS

I'm going to just say it… I hate meetings.

Well, let me clarify. I hate unnecessary and ineffective meetings. Meetings are important for collaboration, communication, and keeping complex projects moving, but when there are too many of them or they aren't run well, they become our top timewaster.

As leaders, effective meetings start with us. I acknowledge that a lot of the meetings we attend aren't ours to control. Many times, we feel like we're being held hostage in a meeting with no hope for escape. However, as leaders of people, there usually are meetings that we arrange and have direct control over. I'd like to share eight tips to keep your meetings on track and productive. I encourage you to find ways to influence others who host meetings in your organization with these ideas as well.

First, it's important to always have a written purpose and agenda prepared and sent out in advance. This allows people to determine *if* they need to be there, and if so, to show up with the necessary work done to be a productive participant in the meeting.

Second, consider scheduling shorter meetings. Sometimes having a 30-minute time slot creates an urgency to stay on track. This allows you to remind tangent-takers and rabbit-trailers that the meeting ends soon, and we need to stay focused on the task at hand. You might also consider a 45-minute block, to allow for transition time to the next meeting.

Third, control the clock. Be vigilant about time boundaries. Start the meeting on time and end it on time. When hosting a meeting, give permission for people to leave at the scheduled time. If you are an attendee at someone else's meeting, protect your valuable time by politely excusing yourself at the published end time, even if the meeting is not over. I recommend that you communicate your "hard stop" at the start of the meeting, so the host is aware that you'll be stepping out at the predetermined time.

Fourth, don't "over-collaborate." Think through who's really required in the meeting and who should be optional.

Sometimes, in the name of collaboration, we include everyone even remotely involved in the meeting topic, even though a few key players may be all that's necessary to accomplish the goal. We often try to avoid offending people by overdoing the invitation list. We think about egos and turf battles, and just decide it's safer to invite everybody.

Instead, make attendance optional for some. When in doubt, reach out to some and let them know your intentions, and that you'll be sure to send a brief report of any decisions and action items coming out of the meeting. That way, people won't feel the need to attend *just in case* something of interest comes up.

Fifth, use a "parking lot" list to avoid time-killing rabbit trails, debates, and work that's better done outside the meeting. A parking lot is just a list of things that really shouldn't take time away from the main purpose of the meeting. Use a flip chart, white board, or just take notes to be sure those issues aren't lost as you move on past them. Documenting those issues so they won't be lost or forgotten will allow people to relax and focus on the current topic.

Sixth, do work outside of the meeting! A big problem with meetings is that people will see one scheduled on their calendar and wait for that timeslot to think about the issue or work on things that could be done individually. As a leader, ensure that individual or smaller group work is being done between larger group meetings. Get commitment on assignments to be completed *before* the next meeting.

Seventh, consider making your meetings a technology-free experience by prohibiting open laptops and phone usage. This will obviously be unpopular with many. Some will even claim that they take all their notes on their tablet, laptop, or phone. If that's the case, then get a group agreement that all non-emergency emails and text messages will be ignored until the end of the meeting.

There's nothing worse than having a room full of people checking and responding to email, texting, or "multi-tasking" on some other issue while the meeting is going on. While this will date me a bit, I call this phenomenon the "blackberry prayer," as everyone sits around the table, heads bowed, hands in their lap, engaged in smartphone use rather than listening to the conversation in the room. If the meeting is worth having, it's worth having everyone's full attention.

Finally, don't leave the meeting without action items and deliverables assigned. As I mentioned earlier, the way to make the meeting worthwhile is to make sure that solid progress happens outside of the meeting. Documenting action items, who's responsible, and when they're due is critical. If you find it difficult to identify specific action items at end of the meeting, you may need to revisit your meeting strategy and make adjustments to be sure progress is being made in future meetings.

There is a plethora of great tools and techniques to ensure that we maximize our most precious resource—time. In this chapter, I've highlighted just a few: focus, prioritization, and meeting control.

The main point to understand is that being a leader requires that we "own" our time. "Lead" is an action verb, and actions take time to complete. Being a leader requires us to commit to doing real-life, everyday supervisory tasks. This book will discuss several of those specific things, including:

- adjusting for personality and readiness,
- ensuring respect,
- planning and goal setting,
- assessing and selecting talent,
- delegating responsibility,
- providing feedback and coaching,
- assisting with change,
- dealing with conflict, and
- developing and challenging our people.

All these tasks take *time*. If we don't protect this valuable resource, we won't be there for our people. Our leadership will be characterized by good intentions and not action.

And that's not leading at all.

THREE POINTS, FIVE QUESTIONS, AND ONE ACTION

Three Points to Review

- It takes real time to do the tasks of leadership, and it's a limited and non-renewable resource to be guarded carefully.

- We make the most of our time by focusing on the most important things and reducing distractions when we do.

- We can instantly multiply our available time to lead by protecting ourselves from meaningless and ineffective meetings.

Five Questions to Ask

1. Am I letting the "tyranny of the urgent" distract me from my most important duties?

2. Do I carve out a little time each day to focus, reflect, and concentrate without interruption?

3. Are the meetings I lead organized, efficient, and resulting in clear action items?

4. Do I treat every hour like the precious, non-renewable resource that it is?

5. Am I prioritizing the tasks and to-dos that my people need from me as their leader?

One Action to Take

✓ Look at your calendar right now and choose at least one recurring meeting that you may be able to eliminate from your schedule. Then do it.

4 UNDERSTANDING PEOPLE

Imagine a world where everything came in only one size. What if clothing stores sold only one size shirt: a women's medium? Sure, that would be great for a few of you...but for the rest of us, that would not be a pretty picture.

How about another example. Imagine you're a handyman or handywoman. Your job is to deal with whatever needs to be fixed, painted, or installed. However, you're only given one tool: a hammer.

Need to pound something in? Great. No problem. Need to cut a piece of wood? Well, you can guess how well that's going to go...

One-size-fits-all doesn't work well with clothing, and one tool isn't enough for all the situations that a handyman or woman faces. When it comes to leading people, using only one style or approach doesn't work either.

People come in a wide variety of personality types. They also have vastly different capabilities and commitment levels. That means that *how* we lead each person on our team will have to be customized to the needs of each individual. Moreover, how we lead each person will often require variety depending on the situation at hand.

Using our *one* favorite leadership "tool" or style with every employee in every circumstance just doesn't work over the long term. While using our favorite "hammer" may get some temporary results, this approach will eventually wear our people out, resulting in lower performance, higher anxiety, and increased turnover. As someone once said, if our favorite tool is a hammer, everything looks like a nail.

While it's true that every person is unique, it's possible to observe patterns in behavior and then classify them using a couple of different simple assessments: their *personality* type and their *readiness* level. Once we have even a basic understanding of these, we can adjust our leadership style and approach to be more effective on an individual basis.

PERSONALITY TYPES

As you may have gathered from the second chapter, I'm a big fan of personality typing systems. I've studied many of the popular ones, like the *Myers-Briggs Type Indicator (MBTI)*, the *Enneagram*, DISC, and others. There's a wide variety of tests and classifications, but most have a common ancestor and have similar properties.

If you have a favorite personality model, use the one you're most comfortable with to understand your people.

However, the one I prefer is the DISC. I've found that it's one of the simplest to grasp and apply to our work and personal lives.

Several years ago, I pursued certification and became an Authorized Partner for Wiley's Everything DiSC® model. Not all DISC assessments are created equal. There are several versions available on the market today, but not all are as rigorously tested and validated as Wiley's Everything DiSC® tool.

This assessment points to four main personality styles, each with three regions. The four main styles are: Dominance, Influence, Steadiness, and Conscientiousness. All styles are equally valuable, and everyone tends to be a blend of all four styles. A person's personality type can be influenced by many factors, including childhood experiences, education, maturity, personal or spiritual transformation, and trauma. This makes personality typing helpful and interesting, but not necessarily fool-proof. Still, after reaching adulthood, our core personality type remains largely consistent over time.

The main point I'd like to make in this short overview of personality is that each type has a pretty consistent set of strengths, priorities, motivations, fears, and limitations. This can be helpful in gaining insight into what might be making an employee "tick" in a given situation.

Knowing the personality type of an employee helps you know what comes naturally to them, and what might take more effort and energy for them. Understanding this can guide our communication, coaching, delegating, and more.

To demonstrate the power of personalities on

behavior, I'll briefly summarizing the four main DiSC types.

Dominance (D)

People with the D style tend be strong-willed individuals who prioritize the bottom line and are driven to achieve results. They value action and are usually pretty focused on getting stuff done quickly and efficiently. They can come across as impatient and are often described as direct and forceful in their communication style. They are typically eager for you to assign them ambitious tasks and have no problem tackling a challenge. They tend to be internally motivated and probably don't require much encouragement.

Influence (i)

I should pause briefly here and explain why Wiley's Everything DiSC® product uses a lower-case "i" for Influence. During my training to become an Authorized Partner, this question came up. Legend has it that the lower-case letter was originally a typo in costly printed marketing materials. Rather than discard the materials, they were used and the small "i" in DiSC has become a trademark of this particular version of the assessment. It can be used to check to see if the tool you use is the research-backed Wiley product that I love so much. So, what about these creatures called "i" types?

People with the i style are generally upbeat and optimistic. They prioritize enthusiasm, action, and collaboration. They're social, expressive, and appreciate giving and receiving encouragement. Often considered the life of the party, they are sometimes distracted by new and different ideas, don't tend to push as hard for bottom line results, and may need some prodding to stay on track.

Steadiness (S)

People with the S style are typically accommodating and flexible. They place a high priority on providing support and tend to be good listeners. They like to help when they can and really value a warm, calm environment. They accept direction easily and will seldom push for more authority. Sometimes, they are so intent on avoiding confrontation that they keep important concerns to themselves. They may need more hands-on support and urging from you to share their ideas.

Conscientious (C)

Team members with the C style relate best to logical objectives and fact-based ideas. They strive for quality results, taking the time to analyze and examine. They prioritize accuracy and stability, and are usually willing to challenge ideas that don't measure up to their standards. They're usually very comfortable working alone and may tend to isolate themselves. C's respond well to tasks requiring careful attention to detail and prefer to be given time and space to produce their best work.

From these simple descriptions, you can see that understanding the personality types of your people can really help as you work to drive results and keep the team functioning in a healthy way. For example, these insights into individuals' motivations, tendencies, and needs can help you manage your time as a leader, or spot communication issues before they become a crisis.

A Simple Personality Assessment

Before we can understand and adjust to our team members' personalities, we obviously need to try to figure out which type they are. The best solution is to utilize the full assessment available for purchase through wolfprairie.com. However, in lieu of a full Everything DiSC® assessment, I'm going to demonstrate how you can do a simple technique which I've found to be about 90% accurate for placing a person in one of the four DiSC styles.

First, rate the person on a vertical axis ranging from "Fast Paced & Outspoken" at the top to "Cautious & Reserved" at the bottom. (See Figure 2.0)

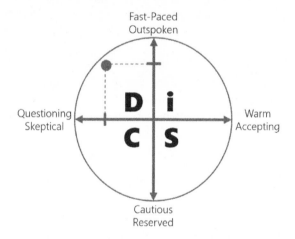

Figure 2.0

Second, rate the person on a horizontal axis ranging from "Questioning & Skeptical" on the left to "Warm & Accepting" on the right.

Third, place a dot where the two ratings intersect. This is the most likely DiSC style of the individual.

While certainly not as reliable as the formal

assessment, I've found the dot placement technique to be a pretty decent approximation for the real thing. It's at least good enough to make some assumptions as you contemplate how best to lead the individual. Using this as a starting place, you should be able to find free resources on the internet that will describe each type in some detail.

READINESS

Our second technique for understanding your people is based on the idea that the "readiness" of a person for a task dictates the most appropriate leadership approach.

The idea that leaders need to adjust their leadership styles and techniques based on specific situations and employee development levels is not new. It's a time-tested philosophy that has been shown to produce excellent results.

My approach to the idea of adaptive leadership is to assess something I call the employee's "readiness." To assess readiness in any given situation, we look closely at two things: an employee's *willingness* and *ability* for the task or project being considered.

A Simple Readiness Assessment

To assist leaders with an easy way to understand and apply this principle, we use what we call the *Wolf Prairie Willing and Able Assessment™*. In this simple back-of-the-napkin assessment, we evaluate a person using another two-scale process. This time, however, our two scales are presented slightly differently. The Willingness scale is on the bottom axis, and the Ability scale is on the left. (See Figure 3.0)

A person's willingness is measured by considering two items: Confidence and Commitment. In this case, the person must show both qualities to be considered fully "willing." They are confident in their knowledge and ability to perform, and they show commitment to getting it done. With only one or the other, they will not be rated as highly on the scale.

Likewise, a person's ability is measured by considering two items: Knowledge and Skills. As with willingness, the person needs both items to be considered fully "able" for the task, project, or assignment. They need both the technical knowledge and demonstrated skills gained through experience to do whatever it is we're going to assign them.

To identify a person's readiness, we do as we did with personality typing, and plot them on both axes, placing a dot where the two lines intersect. This dot placement will fall into one of four boxes.

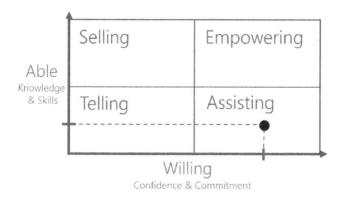

Figure 3.0

Four Leadership Approaches

Depending on the results of our readiness assessment, we'll need to embrace one of four general leadership approaches. I label these approaches as: Telling, Selling, Assisting, or Empowering.

The Telling approach is used when an employee is *neither willing nor able*. When a person falls into this lower left box, we don't leave things to chance. In this approach, we're sure to be more directive and explicit about what, when, and how to do something. Remember, even though this category may sound like a negative one, it could be the result of simple inexperience. For example, a new employee may lack the experience and the confidence to do a particular job early on. Using a Telling approach is necessary until they grow in both willingness and ability over time. This is done for their good and the good of the team.

The Selling approach is used when an employee is *able but not willing*. Perhaps they have the knowledge and skills but seem to be resistant. It's important to note that the lack of willingness is not always a problem with attitude. While that's sometimes the case, at other times, the person just lacks confidence in their own abilities, which can lead to reluctance and resistance. In this approach, we use more persuasion and encouragement to motivate them to get the job done. We spend more time reinforcing their confidence when insecurity is the cause of resistance, and more time convincing and pushing them when hesitance to commit is the issue.

The Assisting approach is used when an employee is *willing but not able*. For example, he or she may have a great attitude and eager willingness, but lack the direct knowledge, skills, and experience to do it alone. I call these types the "Put me in, Coach!" types. It's exciting to see their enthusiasm and confidence, but you realize that there's too much at stake to simply turn them loose. In this approach, we stay more engaged and insist on more involvement and oversight, so the employee can tap into our knowledge and experience when needed.

Lastly, the Empowering approach is used when an employee is *both willing and able*. These employees have the knowledge, skills, confidence, and commitment they need to do the job well. When this is the case, we can happily assign the task or project, get out of the way, and let them run with it on their own. Over time, it should be our goal to develop our people so they all become "Willing and Able" in all the duties of their jobs.

To summarize the main point here, when you're a leader of people at any level, you need to be committed to *studying* your people and employing a variety of leadership approaches and techniques.

Ineffective leaders think, "Well, I'm the boss now. Everybody had better adjust to my style. If they don't like it…there's the door."

An attitude like that is not just ineffective, it's immature! As leaders, more is expected of us. We need to understand our people and adjust our leadership approach as needed. To be an effective, respected, and trusted leader, I urge you to become a *student* of your people.

One size does not fit all.

Real-life leadership requires that we see our people as unique, valuable individuals. This means seeking to first understand them from a core *personality* standpoint, which provides insight into their basic preferences, tendencies, priorities, strengths, limitations, and even fears. Second, we overlay that understanding with clarity about their personal *readiness* to take on a specific assignment or complete their core job duties. That understanding helps the intentional leader to adjust his or her leadership approach to match the situation. This greater understanding and the resulting adaptive leadership will help ensure the team is productive and functioning at the highest level possible.

THREE POINTS, FIVE QUESTIONS, AND ONE ACTION

Three Points to Review

- Leading our people well requires that we recognize them as individuals and seek to understand their motivators, stressors, natural strengths, and inherent limitations.

- Understanding the core personality type of our people allows us to ensure they get from us what they need to be most comfortable and successful at work.

- Assessing whether people are *ready* for an assignment or job duty means making sure they have *both* the willingness and ability they need.

Five Questions to Consider

1. Do I see each person on my team as a valuable, unique individual who wants to be fully known by me?

2. How well do I really know the people reporting to me on a personal level?

3. Am I starting to shift my leadership approach based on each employee's "readiness"?

4. Do I see my people as just "resources" or as "relationships"?

5. Would I be described as a leader who is devoted to my people?

One Action to Take

✓ Grab a sheet of paper and on one side plot the personality type of each of your team members using Figure 2.0. On the other side plot the overall readiness level of each of them using the Willing & Able™ model depicted in Figure 3.0.

5 PROTECTING AND RESPECTING

Nearly everyone knows the story of Rosa Parks' famous refusal to move to the back of a bus in 1955. But most people don't know about another confrontation she had with that same bus driver twelve years earlier.

On a cold day in 1943, Rosa Parks entered the front of that bus and paid her fare. But then the driver told her to leave the bus and enter through the rear doors rather than walk through the bus to her seat in the back. Rosa refused to comply with that rule and ultimately just left the bus and walked, rather than give in.

Twelve years later, her more famous refusal sparked a movement that changed America.

So why do I tell you this story?

Rosa is an icon of determination that became famous because of a failure of leadership. It took the courage of one small, African American woman to rise up and take a stand against injustice and unfair treatment. While we commend her bravery, we can also admit that had elected leaders historically acted in a way that protected and respected *all* people, we wouldn't have needed one of the victims of injustice to rise up at all.

As leaders, we have a special obligation and responsibility to protect our employees and treat them with equality and respect. One of the ways we do this is to do our part to keep them safe from unfair or inappropriate practices and behaviors, such as those that make them feel uncomfortable or prevent them from doing their best work.

THE "COMPLIANCE TRAP"

Most organizations provide "compliance training" to employees and managers covering things like sexual harassment. Many others even attempt to address issues of "diversity" or "inclusion." Unfortunately, many of these programs are treated as "check-the-box" activities, half-heartedly performed at the urging of lawyers or human resource consultants. The company grudgingly provides them, and employees grudgingly sit through them. Sounds like a *really* effective use of time and money, doesn't it?

As leaders of people, it's tempting to see training like this the same way—like just one more corporate-driven waste of time. When we see it this way, we tend to first ignore hidden biases in our own thinking, and then minimize or rationalize them away in others. However, leaders who really lead will see this issue not as a legal requirement, but as a vital consideration for healthy team culture. At the start of this book, I told you that mindset and character are essential to good leadership. Moreover, in the previous chapter, I told you that studying and valuing your people as individuals is another part of effective leadership. The bottom line is, respect is at the foundation of valuing our people, and protecting them from discrimination or harassment is part of our jobs as leaders. This means that this subject can't become merely "check-the-box" lip-service for a true leader; rather, we need to fully grasp the importance of both the legal ramifications and the common-sense applications that we're obligated to understand.

THE LEGAL STUFF

While this is not intended to be a replacement for full training on this subject, I'm going to quickly present the "legal stuff" you need to know as a leader of people. We'll get to the common-sense part shortly, but for now you should also have a sense of the history of these issues and the legal obligations you have as a supervisor, manager, or executive.

Discrimination

Simply put, discrimination is treating someone in some way because of a *group* or category to which they belong, rather than their own *individual* abilities and qualifications.

Here in the United States, we currently have five laws to protect people from discrimination.

1. **The Civil Rights Act of 1964.** This act prohibits discrimination based on race, color, religion, sex, and national origin.

2. **The Age Discrimination in Employment Act of 1967** put in place protections for those aged 40 or older.

3. **The Pregnancy Discrimination Act of 1978** was passed to protect women regarding pregnancy, childbirth, or related medical conditions.

4. **The Americans with Disabilities Act of 1990** came about to protect those with disabilities.

5. **The Genetic Information Non-Discrimination Act of 2008** prohibits using genetic information in health insurance and employment decisions.

These laws have given us what we call "protected categories." This just means that it is illegal to treat someone differently based on any of the categories identified by the five discrimination laws. As of right now, here's the list:

- Race
- Color
- Religion
- National Origin
- Age
- Pregnancy
- Disability
- Genetics

In the workplace, illegal discrimination comes down to this: It's making a decision or impacting a person negatively in some way based on one of those protected categories, rather than on individual merit.

Accommodations

There's one additional related concept I need to mention. Our discrimination laws require that we provide employees with some assistance (an *accommodation*) if asked, for two things: A disability or a sincere religious belief.

In short, if an employee is otherwise qualified to do a job but has a disability or sincere religious belief that limits performance, that employee may request that the employer do something to help.

The law also says that the request should be "reasonable," and less expensive or more feasible options can be offered.

Many of you may not have a human resources department or professional upon which to rely for guidance in this area, so here are a couple of key things you need to know about this.

First, you are not required to *offer* an accommodation or *guess* that someone might need one. Assuming there's a problem and offering or encouraging someone to take an accommodation could be seen as inappropriately drawing attention to the issue and misconstrued as discrimination. The only exception to this is in the case of an obvious need for assistance. If this is the case, gently suggesting that help can be provided might be a better option.

Second, if an accommodation or special assistance is requested, you need to be sure to consider it and engage in discussion with the employee about it. It's during this discussion where the issue can be clarified, and possible alternatives and solutions can be shared. The law requires that employers engage in a dialogue about the disability or sincere religious belief, rather than ignore it or dismiss it out of hand.

If it seems like I'm giving you a lot of citations, lists, legal terms, and detailed instructions, stay with me. In a nutshell, discrimination in any form is not cool. It doesn't really matter if it falls under a specific legal act, or if it's a situation that laws haven't covered quite yet; in all cases, discrimination is inappropriate and has no place in a healthy work environment. So, let's not focus on whether someone is in a formal "protected category." That's not the point. Let's make sure all people, whether they report to us or not, are treated with respect and honor. Let's especially make sure that *our* decisions are all based on objective job requirements, and individual merit, performance, and behavior.

Harassment

Unfortunately, when prejudice, discrimination, and biases exist in the human heart, they come bubbling out in the form of "harassment."

The *illegal* version of harassment is harassing treatment tied to *any* of the protected categories we mentioned earlier.

The most "familiar" form of harassment is *sexual* harassment. It's illegal because it focuses on gender. However, harassment is not limited to gender and can also happen because of race, religion, disability, age, etc.

Technically, there are two types of harassment. The first is called *Quid Pro Quo*. In case your Latin is a little rusty, that means "this for that." This is simply short for, "If you do this for me, I'll do that for you." Quid pro quo harassment is pretty easy to identify. It's manipulation that is performed by a supervisor or anyone with authority in an organization. If this happens even once, it may be grounds for legal action.

The second type of illegal harassment is called *Hostile Work Environment*. This happens when an environment becomes filled with comments, jokes, and behaviors targeting people in any of the protected classes. By the way, a hostile work environment can be created by anyone, not just leaders. It can be created by co-workers, vendors, contractors, and even clients. To meet the legal test of a hostile work environment, the behavior needs to be pervasive and/or severe. A single joke or incident (unless severe) doesn't rise to this level. In any event, leaders have an obligation to intervene and put a stop to it.

So, is all harassment *illegal?*

Technically, no. To be illegal, it would be based on one of those protected categories listed earlier. But let's just agree that all harassment is inappropriate. Let's make it our job as leaders to make sure it doesn't happen on our watch.

Here's the kind of behavior to watch for and eradicate from your team and your culture:

- Bullying
- Verbal abuse
- Intimidation
- Excessive, graphic profanity
- Offensive, mean-spirited comments (even if they are not related to a legally protected category)

This means that harassment aimed at tall people, blondes, young people...or even Ohio State fans is unacceptable in the workplace.

As a leader of people, you need to know that employers have two legal obligations regarding discrimination and harassment. This is important especially if you work in an environment without a significant human resource presence or capability to assist.

Employers (you) need to take reasonable steps to prevent mistreatment, and immediately and thoroughly address a problem if it occurs. Ignoring or dismissing discrimination or harassment, once something is observed or reported, is one of the worst things you can do. If you make this mistake, it's a sure-fire way to lose a lawsuit, and maybe your own job.

Retaliation

In addition to discrimination and harassment, you need to be aware of something called *retaliation*. Retaliation is what happens when someone in authority takes a negative action against someone who has exercised a *protected legal right*.

What's a "protected legal right?" It could be filing a harassment complaint, blowing the whistle on an illegal practice, applying for certain leaves of absence, or even becoming pregnant.

When it comes to retaliation, just know this: Employees are protected by law when they exercise their rights. We as leaders must be very careful to check our attitudes and behaviors when making decisions about employees. If we allow our emotions or frustration with employees to cloud our decision-making, we can easily slip into retaliatory behavior.

Retaliation claims have become very common. It's the fastest growing type of claim filed with the Equal Employment Opportunity Commission (EEOC) and is often attached to any claim of discrimination or harassment. As a supervisor, you need to be *very careful* about this. If you do anything that might be considered to have a negative impact on an employee, you may find yourself the target of a retaliation claim.

Fake Retaliation Claims

What if your "negative" action has nothing to do with a legally protected activity just engaged in by the employee?

Let's face it. Not all employee claims of discrimination, harassment or retaliation are legitimate. Sometimes people are after money or revenge and make false claims.

The secret to avoiding fake retaliation claims is consistent, simple record keeping and documentation. Here are my two documentation rules of thumb:

First, address and document performance and behavior problems right when they occur. Don't do it a week later, once a quarter, or at the end of the year. Do it as soon as possible after you make the observation, or right after you have any sort of "coaching" session.

Second, document your decisions to take action when they're made, even if they won't be implemented until later. This means that if you meet with HR or your boss to discuss something you plan to do regarding an employee, document that decision immediately after you make it even if you don't plan to communicate it or carry it out until the end of the week.

Now, if you're like me and many other leaders of people, you might be saying, "But I don't know how to document something."

Well, fear not. I'm going to share one of my favorite documentation secrets: Email yourself.

Send *yourself* an email documenting the issue, the observation, coaching session, or the decision to make changes or take action. Just pull up an email on your phone or PC, put your name in the "To:" field, jot down a few sentences about the issue, and click Send. Done. If you're an organized type, you can always drag that received email into a special folder for that sort of thing. Otherwise, the search field is your best friend if you need to retrieve that email.

So why email yourself? It's because the timestamp on the email is an all-important piece of evidence. Documenting observations and conversations *when they occur* and decisions *when you make them* can help avoid the appearance of retaliation. It gives you concrete digital evidence to point to if anyone accuses you of reacting to a situation that occurs later.

It takes discipline, but if done right, good documentation only takes a couple of minutes.

The Dos and Don'ts for Leaders

Just to summarize the legal stuff, here are your primary "Dos" as a leader:

1. Model great workplace behavior.
2. Do something immediately if you observe any discrimination or harassment.
3. Get good at documenting everything.

Here are your "Don'ts":

1. Don't discriminate, harass, or retaliate…ever.
2. Don't condone, tolerate, minimize, or ignore it in others.
3. Don't go it alone. Involve your manager, HR, or someone else in leadership.

PROTECTORS AND PREDATORS

Now that you know what law *requires* of you as a leader, I want to briefly appeal to you from a different perspective.

Imagine there were no laws governing how we treat employees? What would our workplaces be like? I'm afraid they would not be very safe or productive places. It's sad that we need government to regulate fair and decent treatment, but that's where the human condition seems to have us.

I believe that there are two types of leaders in the world: Predators and Protectors. There is a lot to this assertion, and too much to cover in this chapter. However, suffice it to say that this distinction drives much of our behavior and priorities as leaders of people.

Here's a basic question to ask yourself: Do I see my employees as objects or people? If our basic lens is one of the predator, we see our jobs, our people, our organizations, our bosses, and our peers as objects to be *consumed*. Predators think first about themselves and their own appetite. Predators don't worry about the well-being of others. They're too focused on getting what's theirs to even see the needs of others.

Protectors, however, see the world differently. They feel a sense of responsibility to create a safe, inviting, and productive space for the people around them. They even feel a sense of warmth and caring about the well-being of their peers and their boss. Protectors are vigilant and always aware of threats in their environment, being willing to step in and act when danger appears. When situations present themselves as a threat to their team's productivity, camaraderie, cohesiveness, and goals, they address them with courage and decisiveness.

When it comes to the things we've discussed in this chapter, protectors act to prevent and respond to them.

Carl

I'd like to wrap up this topic, by telling you a true story about a man named Carl. Carl enjoyed his job as a bus driver until an unfortunate event occurred. He had the misfortune of closely resembling a man that police were after in connection with a rape.

He began to be taunted by coworkers. He was teased and abused with questions like "Who's your next victim, Carl?"

It got so bad that eventually Carl was placed on anti-depressants and medication to lower his blood pressure. He even took time off but returned only to have the abuse and bullying continue.

This continued for some time, until on a cool September day after 22 years of service at the bus company, Carl took his own life.

Where was Carl's supervisor when all this abuse was happening? Why didn't someone in leadership step in to put a stop to it?

With leadership comes responsibility.

It's your responsibility to model great workplace behavior and quickly step in to protect your people. It's tempting to avoid these issues because stepping into one of these situations can be uncomfortable, unpleasant, and sometimes embarrassing. However, *real leadership happens when we do things that we don't feel like doing.*

You're accountable for the well-being of your people. By taking this stuff seriously, you protect them, you protect yourself, and you protect your organization.

THREE POINTS, FIVE QUESTIONS, AND ONE ACTION

Three Points to Review

- As a leader you need to model great workplace behavior and resist the temptation to let familiarity lead to inappropriate words or actions.

- We have laws on the books to protect employees, and it's smart to know what rises to level of illegal activity at work.

- Your people rely on you to be a protector. It takes courage to step in and intervene when people are being mistreated.

Five Questions to Consider

1. Would my team say they feel respected and free to be themselves here?

2. Is there any behavior going on around me that I need to address?

3. Am I documenting my observations, conversations, and coaching sessions as soon as I have them?

4. Am I modeling great behavior and respect?

5. Have I responded to all complaints or calls for help from my team?

One Action to Take

✓ At your next staff meeting, tell your team that you are committed to making your workplace one of respect and honor. Ask them if there's anything at all you need to do about your own behavior or the behavior of others in the work environment.

6 CHARTING THE COURSE

"O.K. We'll go."

Those were the words of Supreme Allied Commander Dwight D. Eisenhower on the morning of June 5th, 1944.

Those words set into action the most massive military undertaking the United States has ever known. He made that statement after careful consideration of the weather situation that threatened to either destroy the operation or delay it for many weeks.

After two full years of planning, the Allied invasion of Nazi-occupied Europe, "Operation Overlord," was finally underway.

It boggles the mind to think about the planning that went into the execution of that D-Day invasion. To name just one element, *Popular Mechanics* magazine reported that more than 125 million maps were used to perfect the master invasion plan.[4]

It was a plan that included 130,000 soldiers, 20,000

---

[4] *How the Invasion Was Planned*, Popular Mechanics magazine, August 1994.

paratroopers, about 7,000 ships, and almost 12,000 aircraft, all perfectly scripted to orchestrate a decisive blow to Nazi Germany in western Europe.

Clearly, none of us will ever be involved in planning something on the scale of the D-Day invasion. But I hope we can agree that the important things in our personal and professional lives deserve some intentional planning and attention.

As leaders at any level, we need to "chart a course" for our teams. We need to be sure our teams know what's most important, where we're going, and how to get there.

Why is this important? Why do we need our people to have clarity about this? Because without it, our teams are at the mercy of the complexity, competing demands, and information overload that happens in every organization.

Without clear vision, strategy, and goals, we see knee-jerk reactions and non-essential urgencies take over. As a result, getting the most important things done successfully is at risk. This is why companies fail, teams underachieve, and even families fall apart.

There's a Japanese proverb that says, "Vision without action is a daydream, and action without vision is a nightmare." It's the nightmare of missed expectations and failed objectives that we want to avoid by charting a course for our teams.

THE ELEMENTS OF CHARTING A COURSE

To unpack the process of charting a course for your team, it's important to define a few terms. Your organization may use different terms for vision-setting and strategic planning. That's okay. The terms used are less important than having them well-defined and consistently applied within your team. Without clarity regarding what you call them, it's difficult to rally around them and communicate effectively.

For now, I'll share the terms I like to use for the components in this process and how they work together: Vision, Strategy, and Goals.

Vision

"Vision" is a desired end state. It's an imagined future condition for the organization or team. Think of it as the main thing the team aspires to achieve or deliver. For you Star Trek fans, it's the prime directive.

A vision doesn't have to be lofty. It can be pretty simple and concrete. For instance, if your team exists primarily to provide quality control in a laboratory environment, your vision might be: *To ensure 100% accuracy and compliance with all regulatory requirements.*

It clearly communicates the main objective of the department. As other demands creep in and things get confusing or chaotic, this statement can act as a point upon which to fix the gaze of the team.

Here's an example of how a vision statement can be used in the context of a project: *The successful completion of Project A by February 1st.*

It describes the desired end state. It paints a clear picture of the ultimate measure of success: A successfully completed project on or before February 1st. Whenever focus wavers, it calls the attention back to the important due date that has been set.

Strategy

"Strategy" is the set of priorities and focus areas that shape the *path* toward the vision. Strategy is where we define the structure, processes, and guidelines that will keep us on track to achieve the vision.

Think of strategy as the map that keeps us on the right track to our destination. Without this "path-shaping" set of priorities, we and our team may wander around, taking a circuitous route to our envisioned destination.

Strategy is not just identifying what we'll focus on to reach our vision, it's also identifying what we *won't* focus on as well. That might be a new way of thinking for you. Have you ever listed the detours and distractions that you plan to *avoid* as you move through your journey?

One important thing to mention is that before you can follow any map, you need to know where you are now. Think about that big red "you are here" arrow on the old rest area bulletin board. So, you may need to gather some data or feedback to clearly know your starting point. Once you know where you are, you can create the strategy to get to your destination.

Vision and strategy are both important, but there's a priority distinction between them. Vision always comes first. *Always*. If you have a clear vision, you will eventually attract the right strategy. If you don't have a clear vision, not even a beautifully crafted strategy will get you where you want to go.

Goals

"Goals" are the measurable objectives we set to ensure we stay on the path to our destination. They're the milestones that reassure us that we'll arrive at the correct location at the right time.

This is where the numbers come in.

Goals are detailed enough to measure our progress along the way and tell us whether we've achieved our vision at the end. Embarking on a strategic journey to a visionary destination without clear objectives and milestones is not effective. Having a vision and strategy, without goals, is throwing caution to the wind, hoping for the best. It's like beginning a long sea voyage having no idea how much food and water need to be loaded on board.

Okay, let me just summarize the elements of the plan.

- Vision is the desired end state or future condition for the team.

- Strategy is the set of structures, priorities, and focus areas to shape the path toward the vision.

- Goals are the measurable objectives to ensure we stay on the strategic path toward our vision.

When we have these three things in place, we have effectively "charted a course."

TRUE NORTH

Most of us lead teams that fit into a larger organization. We may lead a department. We may be a supervisor in a plant or laboratory. We may manage a team of salespeople.

So, is it possible to chart a course for our team when

we're part of a larger entity that has its own vision or mission?

The short answer is "yes."

The longer answer is still yes, but you need an understanding of what I call "True North."

True North is a navigational concept that refers to an imaginary line running through the Earth. This is different from magnetic north, which is calculated using a compass. You see, True North never changes, but magnetic north is constantly changing slightly, depending on where you are on the globe.

Author Bill George says that "True North is your orienting point. Your fixed point in a spinning world."

In our context, True North is your organization's own vision, purpose, values, and top objectives. Our efforts to chart a course for our teams must align with the vision, strategy, and goals of the larger organization. Otherwise, our plans may conflict with the top priorities of the organization as a whole.

This of course means we need to know what those top priorities, values, and objectives are at all times. If we're unsure, or can't easily describe what these things are, we need to seek clarity from above until we have our "True North" firmly established.

CREATING ALIGNMENT AND ACCEPTANCE

Of course, even the best plans will fail if people don't support them and play their parts. So how do you ensure that your team is on board and willing to stick to the plan?

You involve them.

A plan created by the leader is the leader's plan. A plan created with team involvement, ideas, and feedback is the team's plan. It ensures that all are aligned on what's most important and why. It also ensures that potential problems and barriers are foreseen and planned for accordingly.

Admittedly, we all serve at the pleasure of someone else. So not all elements of your charted course may be up for discussion. In those cases, explaining rationale to your team, checking for understanding, and asking for commitment is still important.

GET YOUR HEAD OUT OF THE BOAT

There's an expression among sailboat racers (although I am not one of them) that calls for sailors to "get your head out of the boat."

There comes a time after all the basic data has been gathered for the course, like wind speed, boat speed, compass direction, etc., when we need to adjust the plan based on whatever else is happening on the racecourse. Things like other boats, unexpected obstacles, and changing wind direction, just to name a few.

This just means that after our planning is complete and the plan is underway, we need to get our head out of the boat and observe and respond to the reality happening before us.

Helmuth von Moltke, a nineteenth-century German field marshal, once said, "No battle plan survives contact with the enemy."

A more recent example of this idea comes from boxer Mike Tyson, when he said, "Everyone has a plan until he gets punched in the face."

This just means that even the best laid plans tend to go awry when they come into violent contact with something called *reality*. When plans and reality collide, reality doesn't yield. It's the plan that must change.

Establishing a vision, creating a strategy, and documenting goals is *not* a once-and-done exercise. Once the course has been charted, we need to be sure to revisit it often, ensuring that reality hasn't rendered the plan inoperable.

I started this chapter talking about Dwight Eisenhower, the architect of perhaps the greatest plan in history. He also said something about planning which at first glance seems counterintuitive. He said, "In preparing for battle, I have always found that plans are useless, but planning is indispensable."

I think the point he was making is that the process of planning, discussing, preparing, goal setting, and getting everyone aligned around purpose was critical for when the plans were rolled out. He knew that the original details of the plan wouldn't survive reality, but the planning process was necessary to be ready to respond to changing circumstances.

I hope you see and agree that charting a course with and for your team is a critical function of leading others. It can and should be done by all of us, whether we supervise a group of people pushing brooms, lead an entire company, or something in between.

Don't wait for your organization or department head to hand out strategic assignments and goals for your team.

In most cases, that will never happen. Instead, make sure *you* set aside the time to chart a course for your people by defining a vision, establishing a strategic path, and setting solid goals to be sure you stay on track to achieve your team's primary purpose.

THREE POINTS, FIVE QUESTIONS, AND ONE ACTION

Three Points to Review

- Your people need you to be purposeful in planning and create a sense of purpose and organization to help them make sense of the chaos around them.

- Establishing a vision, creating a strategy, and documenting goals doesn't need to be daunting or complex. Simple is better and easier to rally around.

- Don't fall so much in love with your plan that you miss the evolving landscape and ignore warning signs calling for a change.

Five Questions to Consider

1. Can my people verbalize our team's core vision (the prime measure of success), or do I need to simplify it?

2. Have I clarified our strategies or focus areas for achieving that vision?

3. Are the goals we've established aligned and "SMART" (specific, measurable, achievable, relevant, and time-bounded)?

4. Is my head still in the boat, or am I open to scrapping my plans if data tell me it's not working?

5. Do I have my team's support for our plan or are they secretly disengaged because I failed to include them on how we'll get where we're going?

One Action to Take

✓ At your next staff meeting, ask the team to write down (individually) what they think your team's main objective or prime directive is. Then compare them and start the discussion to clarify your vision.

7 SELECTING PEOPLE

We've all heard the expression that a chain is only as strong as its weakest link. A chain can have a thousand strong links, but if one of those links is weak, the entire chain is useless.

Interestingly, when a chain, or a bridge, or anything else lacks *strength*, it can't be trusted and is said to lack *integrity*.

Besides having integrity, a chain must also be fundamentally designed to handle the job at hand. Even a solid, well-designed, one-inch chain link is a bad fit for the job of securing an ocean freighter to a pier. A one-inch steel chain link simply doesn't have the fundamental attributes for that purpose. All the integrity in the world won't make that chain successful.

I find this to be a great analogy for selecting people for our teams. Choosing an ill-fitting or weak team member affects the success of the entire team.

The challenge we face as leaders is that it's actually really hard to truly assess candidates using a resume and a couple of interviews. On the surface, a candidate may seem to have all the right experience, skills, and attributes. It's not until we assess the inner strength and intangible capabilities that we can truly understand the strength and job fit of that potential link in our chain.

The good news is that there are some good strategies and tools to make better selection decisions.

This is important because the true cost of a bad hire is staggering. There is a lot of variation in the literature about how to estimate the cost of replacing a bad hire. The actual cost depends on the type of position, authority level, and the industry involved. Suffice it to say that just the *direct* expenses to recruit, interview, onboard, and train the wrong person are significant.

It's the *indirect* costs that are harder to estimate and even more destructive. The damage to culture, cost of co-worker morale, drops in customer satisfaction, loss of productivity, missed organizational objectives…and the list goes on.

While it takes more time to strategically and carefully select someone for your team, it's one of the most important things you can do for your organization and the rest of your people.

Benjamin Franklin once said, "An ounce of prevention is worth a pound of cure." He was talking about fire safety, but when it comes to selecting people for your team, this couldn't be truer.

In this chapter, I'm going to quickly address the following strategies and tips for selecting people:

- Preparation before a candidate search.

- Preparing for each interview.

- Using a variety of question types.

- The importance of intangibles.

PREPARING FOR A SEARCH

I often see leaders jump right into the hiring process without much planning or preparation. Very little time is spent carefully considering the candidate requirements and attributes most needed for the position.

To make matters worse, if this step is skipped, others involved in the hiring decision often have differing ideas about the job's requirements and what is needed to ensure a good candidate fit. I've seen selection processes grind to a halt as interviewers disagree about which candidate is the best fit.

Using a simple list of clearly defined *selection criteria* can create alignment among evaluators before the process is started. It gets everyone measuring candidates using the same measuring stick. This can be done by simply listing the three to five most important criteria for selection, defining them, and then asking all interviewers to evaluate candidates on those items using a common scale. This reduces a lot of the inherent subjectivity and introduces a little science into the selection process. Failure to do this tends to result in a lot of future finger pointing if a hiring decision turns out badly.

Beware of the Icing on the Cake

As you prepare your final list of selection criteria, it's important to avoid the shiny object syndrome—getting enamored by a candidate's "icing on the cake" qualifications.

I've seen this as supervisors choose candidates because of some additional characteristic or qualification not required for the position. For instance, if a position requires a bachelor's degree, but a Ph.D. shows interest, it's tempting to "get something for free" and hire the Ph.D. This "icing" may cause you to overlook missing essential ingredients of core experience, skills, or personal attributes needed for the job.

Someone once said that there's no such thing as a free lunch. It's true. Hiring someone with extraordinary qualifications for the same price as someone without them usually produces unwanted results as their feeling of "under-employment" begins to fester and emerge over time.

So, focus on the cake's core ingredients of experience, education, and personal attributes, and go lightly on the icing.

PREPARING FOR EACH INTERVIEW

While we're on the topic of preparation, let me encourage you to prepare for each interview you have. There is a *lot* to assess when you conduct an interview, and usually not a lot of time to do it.

Interviewing without a written set of questions is a recipe for a haphazard and ineffective interview. It almost certainly guarantees that what you discover in an interview won't provide the information needed to evaluate the candidate against your selection criteria.

Having a set of questions prepared in advance will

keep you on track in the interview, ensure you get what you need to rate the candidate, and even allow you to finish on time. It's also helpful to tell the candidate that you have a set of questions, and you may need to interrupt or redirect in order to get to all your questions. Explain to the candidate that this is important to ensure consistency with other candidates.

QUESTION TYPES

For the last couple of decades, a certain form of interviewing called *behavioral interviewing* has received almost exclusive attention. This is simply asking the candidate to describe a time from the past that demonstrates experience, skill, or knowledge in a certain area. The theory is that if the candidate can recall circumstances where that skill was used, he or she is likely to do it again in the new position.

However, some people use behavioral interviewing questions exclusively, and I think that's a mistake. First, there's no guarantee that the example is even real. A deceptive candidate will have no trouble concocting a convincing story about their past experiences that has no basis in reality…and there's no real way to fact-check it. So just because someone can explain in detail how they helped resolve a difficult conflict, or solved a challenging problem, or managed a complex project, doesn't mean they really did. Even if they did, it doesn't mean they were successful doing it.

Rather than rely solely on these types of questions, I'd like to encourage you to utilize three additional types of questions in your interview plan.

First, I think there's a place for the *hypothetical*

question. Hypotheticals can help you assess a candidate's ability to quickly apply knowledge or experience to a scenario they may face in the job. For instance, you could ask something like, "If you were presented with such-and-such a situation, what would your thought process be like, and what are the steps you would take to address it?"

While hypothetical questions don't guarantee the candidate has ever done a specific thing, they can tap into the knowledge and understanding someone may have on an issue.

The second type of question is the *unconventional* question. These are questions that throw a candidate off balance, so you can assess things like thinking skills, flexibility, and even sense of humor. Here's one I like: "If you could have dinner with anyone from history, who would it be and why?"

Unconventional questions can also break the ice, cause the candidate to relax, and make the interview process more fun. Answers to these sorts of questions can provide a glimpse into the personality, priorities, and interests of the candidate. Just be careful not to ask questions that cause the candidate to respond with personal information about age, family status, medical history, or the like. If something personal or non-job-related is shared, don't write it in your notes. It's not relevant to the decision you're trying to make, and you don't want to answer awkward questions about why you listed the candidate's number of children or other personal information in your notes.

The third additional question type I'd like to mention is the *challenge* question. Microsoft had some legendary examples, like, "How many golf balls does it take to fill a 747?"

Challenge questions can help you assess a candidate's thought processes, reasoning abilities, and problem-solving skills. It also provides a glimpse into how he or she may respond under pressure.

By the way, the answer is approximately 20,000,000 golf balls, depending on whether the seats have been removed.

The point of all this is to use the interview time to assess as many aspects of the individual as possible. Don't just gather information about past jobs and education which you can easily read about on the resume.

Okay, so now you have a great set of questions that will challenge the candidates and get them to open up a window to who they really are. The big question is, what's more important, straight knowledge and experience, or interpersonal fit, character, and potential?

ASSESSING INTANGIBLES

I've always been a proponent of hiring a great person with solid potential and then training them for any skills that may be lacking. I can teach someone skills. I can help provide people with new knowledge. However, it's much harder to impact an employee's character, integrity, or core relational effectiveness.

Unfortunately, this is much harder to assess in a 30- or 60-minute interview, and reference checks don't often result in any real honest information.

The solution is to get good at using observations and the questioning techniques I just reviewed to get a clearer picture of person's integrity, values, and how they'll interact with others on your team.

Another technique is to ask follow-up questions to dig deeper. Most candidates practice their answers to predictable questions. When you get those canned answers, respond by following up with a question like, "What would you do differently if you could do it again?" or "What did you learn from that?"

Thought-provoking questions and follow-up inquiries can reveal far more about a person than a boring discussion about the job duties performed at the last place of employment.

So, before conducting interviews, take the time to search online for creative questions that can get behind the resume and reveal a candidate's integrity, team mentality, emotional intelligence, and even humility. Find a couple of interesting questions and ask them to each of your candidates for comparison purposes. Then encourage other people in the interview process to do the same.

I'm not suggesting that experience, education, and knowledge are unimportant. They need to be assessed to be sure there is a fundamental job fit. I'm just suggesting that we should also try to assess the quality of the *human* in front of us as well.

I've seen way too many hiring managers select the candidate with the most *experience* or best educational pedigree, only to unwittingly introduce a toxic element into their team that destroys its chemistry and culture. Remember, years of experience do not translate directly to effectiveness in many cases. I hate to say it, but there may be an underlying reason the person is looking for a new job…again.

To recap, you owe it to yourself, your team, and your organization to select strong links for your chain. The cost of a bad hiring decision can be devastating financially and culturally.

First, prepare for the search process by deciding in advance on the most important selection criteria. Get everyone else involved in the process to agree on what they are.

Second, prepare for each interview by reviewing candidate resumes in advance and preparing a list of questions designed to evaluate the candidate on all the selection criteria.

Third, use a variety of questions: behavioral, hypothetical, unconventional, and maybe even throw in a challenge question. Just be sure to avoid "illegal" ones that ask about personal, non-job-related things.

Finally, remember that experience and formal education aren't *everything*. All the experience and education in the world won't make a rotten person a good fit for your team. Use the interview process to get beyond the resume and find ways to assess intangibles.

Look for character quality, integrity, others-focus, problem-solving abilities, critical thinking skills, emotional intelligence, a team mentality, and even humility. If you're going to be training the new hire to fill in skill gaps, you might want to look for *teachability* as well.

Investing the time to carefully evaluate and select the right *humans* for your team is one of the most important responsibilities of leadership. Even if your selection will require additional training or time spent with you to become proficient, choosing good people with good potential is always the best decision.

One bad apple *can* spoil the whole barrel.

THREE POINTS, FIVE QUESTIONS, AND ONE ACTION

Three Points to Review

- The decision to place someone on your team has more impact on culture and results than almost anything else you do.

- Each link in your chain must have the integrity and core capabilities to fulfill its purpose. Any weak link has the potential to render the chain useless.

- We need to use creative (legal) questions to assess intangibles so we can get past the resume to find the best *human* possible for the position.

Five Questions to Consider

1. Is it possible that I've relied too much on resume experience or educational credentials when selecting among a list of candidates?

2. Have I let "nice-to-haves" distract me from evaluating the right criteria?

3. Has conventional wisdom about using just "behavioral interviewing" limited my approach?

4. The next time I hire, am I prepared to evaluate candidates using a defined set of criteria that

balances experience with core attributes?

5. If I've selected a good *human* with a skill gap or two, do I need to do any extra training or coaching to shore up capabilities?

One Action to Take

✓ Consider each person on your team as a link in a chain and honestly evaluate if any are creating frailty and limiting your team's effectiveness. Then do something to help them.

8 GETTING STUFF DONE

What's the most basic reason for leadership? Not the definition of leadership…the *reason* for it. Think about it. Why do we put people in charge of other people in the first place?

I propose that the most basic duty of a leader is to get stuff done through people. It is why organizations are *organized* into groups with individuals given responsibility over those groups. The alternative is having everybody trek into work looking for direction and answers from the owner or founder of the organization. This would not be a pretty sight as the number of people grows.

In fact, this model has been around for thousands of years. Moses, the famous Israelite leader and prophet, started to use this system after his father-in-law intervened in the chaos and said, "Dude, you're killing yourself, and the people ain't happy either… Instead, put some trusted people over groups of thousands, hundreds, fifties, and tens." (Exodus 18:18, 21 – DeWolf Version)

Seriously, isn't the true measure of a leader's core success the ability to deliver results through the human resources assigned?

EMPOWERMENT AND DELEGATION *YAWN*

To break down how to get stuff done through your people, I'm going to blow the dust off a concept that everyone talks about, but few execute properly.

It's the idea of *empowerment*.

Stay with me. I realize this word is very 1990s. I know that it has gone the way of many popular business buzzwords. It's become just that: a buzzword, largely devoid of practical meaning.

So, ironically, to revive the idea of empowerment, I'm going to blow even more dust off another term that's much older and even more familiar to all of us: *delegation*.

Delegation comes from the word "delegate," obviously. In the verb form, it means to *entrust a task or responsibility to another person.*

So why would I waste space in a small book on leadership to stress the importance of this simple and commonplace daily activity? Because this seemingly mundane task is much more important than most people realize.

First, forget everything you think you know about delegation. We're going to relearn what it means and how to delegate properly to get great stuff done through your people, essentially *empowering* them to work without your direct involvement.

We're going to talk about three things: preparation,

treating the delegation conversation as a formal event of sorts, and debriefing after the delegated task is complete.

By the way, delegating well is not only a tool to get results. It also creates job satisfaction by providing growth opportunities, increases autonomy, and, if done well, can even reduce anxiety in your people.

PREPARATION

At first glance, delegating seems straightforward. I mean, don't you just pull somebody aside, assign a task, and move along?

It's tempting to just forward an email as our "process" of delegation. Click. Done. Move on.

Bad idea.

As with most things, a lack of planning will result in confusion and missed expectations. Like everything else, it seems, properly delegating something requires at least some preparation by the leader. So, what do we need to do?

Preparing to delegate is a three-step process. First, we document the deliverables and deadlines. Second, if we have a choice, we select the *right* delegate. Third, we identify the constraints, or what I call the "navigational buoys."

Deadlines and Deliverables

It's important to think in advance and write down the specific deliverables and deadlines for the task or project you're about to assign. What are the timelines? What's the measure of success? How do you know when it's fully complete?

Thinking these things through in advance, and writing them down, will ensure that a complete message is sent to the person receiving the instruction.

Choose Your Delegate

Next, based on the deliverables and deadlines you just determined, make sure you've selected the *right* person for the task you're about to assign. Do this by thinking through the readiness of the individual. Is he or she both willing and able to handle the task or project? Where might the person struggle? What do they need from you to be successful?

By doing this, you may reconsider to whom you want to assign the task, or at a minimum you can adjust your own expectations about how much detail to provide and how involved you'll need to be.

Identify Navigational Buoys

The last step of preparation emerges from your work in the first two steps. You need to identify the *navigational buoys*. Buoys are the guidelines, time limits, budgets, and other non-negotiables for the task or project. Again, you need *write them down*.

Here's why I call these constraints, "buoys." Real buoys ensure safe travel along the voyage to a destination. When we stay between the navigational buoys, we can relax and enjoy the journey. Buoys are our friends. They allow the individual discretion on how to accomplish the task you're assigning, while making sure they stay on course.

Buoys are those constraints and limits within which a person is permitted to navigate and make decisions. Buoys help the employee avoid danger zones that could result in failure.

Those are the three steps involved in preparing to delegate. Doing these things in advance will ensure an effective hand-off from you to the person receiving the request.

THE DELEGATION CONVERSATION

I really want to encourage you to avoid the nonchalant acts of delegation. You know the kind. The hastily forwarded email, or the "oh-by-the-way" hallway conversation.

Instead, consider a more *formal* delegation conversation. Think of it as a short kick-off meeting of sorts.

You're probably saying, "Oh great, another meeting I don't have time for." However, if you've prepared in advance, this can be a five- or ten-minute conversation that creates clarity, commitment, and results. Skipping it will probably require more time down the road as questions are asked and errors are corrected.

The delegation conversation should focus on two things: details and dialogue.

Details

When you think about what details you should share, I recommend you consider four things: explaining the "why," sharing the deliverables and deadlines, describing the navigational buoys, and setting up checkpoints.

First, be sure to share the "why." Explain the reason you're asking for something to be done. It's important to put the request into *context*. Doing this helps to build ownership and acceptance.

Second, share the specific deliverables and deadlines you thought through during your preparation. Clearly illustrate what success looks like. Paint a very clear picture of the finished product and required timelines, so expectations are understood at the outset.

Third, discuss the buoys within which the employee is permitted to navigate. These might be budget constraints, key regulations, laws, or other guidelines, limits, or specifics handed down from above.

Fourth, set up *checkpoints*. Checkpoints are agreed-upon points in time where you will check back in with the person to chat about progress, review work, and answer questions. An example of this is to create a short 15- or 30-minute recurring meeting on the calendar. The more complex the project, or inexperienced the delegate, the more frequent the cadence might need to be.

Checkpoints help ensure that the individual doesn't stray too far from the desired course. Why set up these checkpoints in advance? Because if we don't, they often get neglected completely. There's nothing worse than receiving a fouled-up assignment the day it's due. The result? Chaos and emergency work for you and others.

The more difficult or important an assignment, the more likely it could go awry without the occasional update and redirection that only you as the leader can provide.

Dialogue

It may seem obvious that a "conversation" would have dialogue, but too often, delegation is a monologue. "Here's the project, here's what I need, now get going."

When we think about dialogue, we have three things we want to achieve: checking for understanding, gathering commitment, and helping to reprioritize.

First, check for understanding. We need to ask questions to be sure the assignment is clear and well understood. Some employees are afraid to speak up when they're confused or unclear, because they think they should already know what you're talking about. They may be embarrassed about not understanding what you're saying.

Often, they just nod in agreement and secretly plan to go back and figure things out on their own. This is not a good thing. Not only does it waste time and cause anxiety in the employee, but it can easily result in missed expectations.

The second element of dialogue is gathering commitment and ensuring accountability. Some employees may listen to your request but not fully buy into or even agree with what you're asking. Some will leave a delegation conversation with absolutely no intention of following through. Some will even hope you'll forget that you delegated the assignment to them at all, or act like *you* didn't make it clear that *they* were supposed to do something.

Asking for a commitment can reveal if the person is hesitant, unclear, or resistant to your request. If so, it's well worth your time to spend a few more minutes explaining rationale, understanding concerns, and getting that commitment.

The third element of dialogue involves prioritization. You may need to help your employee reprioritize his workload before you end the conversation.

He may be clear about your request and may commit to doing it, but leave the meeting panicking because of the all the stuff already on his plate.

Taking the time to ask if he has any concerns or needs help shifting priorities can help you get the results you need most, and reduce his stress and anxiety.

DEBRIEFING

Next, I want to quickly mention the importance of debriefing after a completed assignment. Just as we see the delegation meeting as a kick-off "event" of sorts, we should use a debrief meeting to formally wrap it up.

It's a good idea to review the quality, budget, timing, and finished product to be sure the assignment was completed as directed. That way if something's yet to be finished, or needs to be redone, you can redirect the employee to complete the task, and you won't end up doing it yourself.

Another thing I recommend when you debrief after a delegation is to review the delegation process itself. Take the time to listen, and don't be defensive if your team member has feedback about your clarity of direction and delegation.

MICROMANAGEMENT

For many years in workshops and training programs, I've asked participants to describe the *worst* boss they've ever had using the key words, attributes, and traits that come to mind first. I've gathered those responses each time and have several hundred in a database. One of the most commonly selected words has been *micromanager*.

For many of us, our need to be in control or fear of failure can manifest itself in our leadership as micromanagement. Unfortunately, it's one of the leading causes of employee unhappiness. So, we need to be very careful not to cross the line from detailed delegation to overly controlling micromanagement.

I like to check myself in this regard using the buoy analogy described earlier.

Imagine you rent a boat to explore a beautiful intercoastal waterway with your family and friends. Your instruction from the harbor master is to feel free to wander through the channel, staying between the navigational buoys in order to avoid underwater hazards. However, as you leave the pier and begin your voyage, you see a long line of thousands of narrowly spaced buoys. In fact, as you sail, you have just a few feet of space on each side of your boat.

This is what it's like when we as leaders lay out excessive constraints, instructions, and personal preferences, taking all ability to think and reason from our people. As people progress in experience and capability, they want to see an equal progression in your willingness to trust them with autonomy, freedom, and decision-making.

So, watch the number of buoys. Recognize the

capabilities of each team member and assign only the number of buoys necessary to avoid disaster.

PUTTING IT TOGETHER

Let's reassemble the pieces of the delegation puzzle.

First is preparation. It's important to prepare to delegate by thinking through the required deadlines and deliverables, matching the right person to the assignment, and documenting the constraints or "buoys" of the project in advance.

After preparation, you're ready for your delegation conversation. In this "kick off" event, we focus on the two D's of details and dialogue. We share the who, what, where, when, why, and sometimes how of the project or task being assigned. Then we arrange for checkpoints along the way.

Finally, at the completion of the assignment, we debrief by reviewing the results, and maybe even getting a little feedback on our own delegation skills. This is also where we'll learn if we *over-buoyed* them in the process, slipping into micromanagement.

If you recall, the core expectation and measure of success for any leader, at any level, is the ability to get stuff done through people.

It's important that we fully utilize the people assigned to us, maximizing their productivity through the effective distribution of work by *delegating*.

This is what empowerment is all about. Empowering, or delegating, is a critical skill that takes practice and commitment on our part.

Your people crave direction without micromanagement. They need clear and appropriate instruction to feel confident that they're focused on the right things. Knowing and understanding your expectations and the autonomy they have to make decisions provides a welcome relief from a lot of stress and anxiety.

I understand that the demand on our time as leaders is crazy. It's easier to quickly assign tasks or projects and hope for the best. However, short-changing the delegation process will result in a lot of bad consequences. It will cause missed expectations, dropped balls, frustrated and anxious employees, and our own bosses unhappy with *our* performance.

Remember, the core reason we've been entrusted with a leadership position is to empower the people assigned to us to get great stuff done. That's how the organization gets its return on investment in us as leaders.

THREE POINTS, FIVE QUESTIONS, AND ONE ACTION

Three Points to Review

- Getting stuff done through the people assigned to us is the most fundamental reason we have organizational structures and reporting relationships in the first place.

- Careful, thoughtful delegation is imperative to ensure that your expectations are clear, the message has been received, and the right results will follow.

- It's powerful and trust-building when you humbly seek feedback on your delegation skills while you debrief after a delegated assignment is complete.

Five Questions to Consider

1. Do I plan my expectations and requirements before I hand off assignments?

2. Do I tend to lay down so many "buoys" that I remove all freedom and autonomy?

3. Could I be accused of "helicopter" management by hovering over my people, asking for constant updates or opportunities to review their work?

4. Am I retaining tasks for myself because deep down, I don't think others will do them right?

5. Do I remember to circle back to debrief the project before moving on?

One Action to Take

✓ Search your to do list or calendar and select one thing you can delegate to someone on your team today. Then do it. This will create margin in your schedule to do the tasks of leadership.

9 MAXIMIZING RESULTS

"Look at me," she said.

That halted my train of thought, and I stopped talking. I was in a meeting with my boss as part of our performance management process. It was about halfway through the year, and I really wanted a top rating at the end of the year.

When I stopped my rambling about my accomplishments and plans and looked at her, she said this: "Jeff, you have a lot of activity going on, but I need you to focus on what's keeping *me* up at night."

Instantly, I asked what those things were. She explained that she wanted results in two key areas above all else.

Boom. Clarity.

Suddenly, my crazy, multifaceted, competing-demands job was less overwhelming. I knew at that moment that my boss would give me a strong performance rating (and the bigger salary increase that went with it) if I delivered the two things she mentioned.

My work effort changed from that day forward. Each day, I made sure I made progress on those two things. Do you know what else? Much of my anxiety left me, like a weight off my shoulders.

We know that the most fundamental purpose of leadership structure is to get stuff done through people. But just getting stuff done is not enough. Getting stuff done *correctly* and with *maximum results* is just as important.

THE ESSENTIAL INGREDIENT

At first glance, I admit that it seems a bit ambitious to include a chapter on how to maximize results. After all, results are the name of the game. However, as the old adage says, if we want to eat an elephant, we need to do it one bite at a time. Here's the recipe for that first bite.

The essential ingredient in the recipe to maximize results is providing frequent and specific *corrective feedback* to our people.

The process of providing corrective feedback only works if expectations are made crystal clear, as my boss did for me that day. However, growing in the courage and discipline to provide corrective feedback and constructive criticism is an area where most of us have a great need for improvement.

Over the course of my career, I have seen one particular fear the most often in leaders at all levels. While public speaking is a close second, the thing that leaders fear *the most* is giving negative feedback.

Before jumping into this discussion, let me just define

the word *fear*. Many leaders recoil when accused of being afraid. Most of us have been taught, either directly or subliminally, that good leaders are fearless, confident, and heroic. So, when I say that there is a common shared fear among leaders, it's natural to resist.

Leaders will often say, "I'm not *afraid* to do it, I'm just too busy to 'babysit' my people." Or, "I'm not afraid to have difficult conversations, I just don't like them." Or, "My people know when I'm unhappy with performance. I don't need to tell them about it."

These are all examples of *avoidance*. Remember, humans love to avoid things that are unpleasant, uncomfortable, unfamiliar, or painful. We move away from pain and toward comfort.

Avoidance is driven by fear.

Nobody would think less of you for being afraid of a mountain lion in your path and doing what you can to avoid it. If you are afraid to touch a red-hot stove and avoid doing it, you're not a wimp, you're a smart human.

However, when we are told that we fear conflict or providing negative feedback, we get defensive or deny it. We'll only begin to improve as leaders when we start to admit that we avoid things because they scare us or make us uncomfortable. It's because of this tendency that we're going to focus on providing constructive criticism as a critical skill that leaders need to master if they want to maximize results.

ESTABLISH A COACHING CULTURE

So, where do we start?

First, it's important to establish a "coaching culture" on your team. This is simply creating an expectation that there will be corrective feedback. Appeal to your team that everyone (including you) has room for improvement. Making mistakes and receiving corrective feedback is how we improve. It may help to point out that even elite athletes hire coaches to push them and point out where their game needs to improve, not simply to praise them and tell him how great they are.

Essentially, I like to ask for *permission* to coach, while also giving permission *to be coached* on how I'm doing as leader. Obviously, we don't need an employee's actual permission to coach them or provide feedback on their performance. I'm not implying that our workplaces are little democracies. By asking for permission to coach, we're creating mental consent to coaching in advance. We're appealing to their reasonableness in a setting free of emotions and natural primitive brain reactions. (More on that topic in Chapter 11.) This sets the stage, and it can minimize the tendency for people to become defensive.

THE CONSTRUCTIVE FEEDBACK MEETING

Obviously, it's important to do the constructive feedback meeting correctly and effectively.

You're probably familiar with the saying, "Praise in public, criticize in private." This is important.

Getting criticized or "coached" in public can feel humiliating. When we're humiliated or embarrassed, it's much harder (if not impossible) to positively and openly receive the message. So, always hold your corrective feedback meeting in private.

Now, how do you do it?

I'm sure you've heard of the *feedback sandwich*. You know, start with something positive to warm them up, then hit them with the negative stuff you're really there to talk about, then end with something positive that will make them feel better about themselves and not be as mad at you.

Well, forget about that. It's a bad idea that can erode trust, as employees question whether you really meant the positive stuff.

Have a B.L.T.

Instead of the feedback sandwich, I think you should have a feedback B.L.T. Who doesn't love a good B.L.T.? Toasted bread, crisp bacon, fresh lettuce and tomato, topped off with a generous portion of mayonnaise…but I digress.

When it's time to have a difficult conversation about correcting behavior, I want you to think about having a B.L.T. Here's what B.L.T. stands for:

The "B" stands for *be direct*. It's never a good idea to start a corrective feedback conversation beating around the bush. Instead, be direct about why you want to talk right up front. Don't start with a lot of false praise or unnecessary small talk. That just serves to create additional anxiety and can feel fake.

Say something like, "John, I need to talk to you about what happened in that meeting a couple hours ago, because I'm concerned about what you said." When you start the conversation, be direct and clearly say *what* you need to talk about, and *why*.

The "L" in B.L.T. reminds us to *listen*. A corrective feedback conversation should never be a monologue. Listening implies that the person receiving the feedback has a chance to speak as well.

One way to invite dialogue is to admit that you may not have a clear picture about what happened, and that you're interested in their perspective as well. It's important to be open to the chance that you don't see the situation as clearly as you think you do.

Also, ask them to describe the situation as they see it, and ask if they agree with your assessment of the issue. I have found that in most cases, the other person will agree or be even harder on themselves than you're being. In any event, they appreciate the chance to share their reasons or rationale.

Finally, the "T" in B.L.T. stands for *transition*. Since no one wants to spend all day in these sorts of meetings, transition to the next steps, focusing on two things.

First, get commitment about the change needed. In some cases, this is getting a verbal agreement that a behavior won't happen again.

Second, be clear about the consequences of the behavior, if there are any. For instance, they may need to go and fix something or apologize to someone. Or more seriously, there may be some other disciplinary measure, like a suspension, that you need to communicate. It really depends on the severity of the issue you're addressing.

When you think "transition," you should be focused on drawing the conversation to a close and moving on together in a healthy and productive manner.

In short, focusing on the B.L.T. of corrective feedback

can give structure and efficiency to a difficult conversation.

WHEN TO PROVIDE FEEDBACK

So, let's say one of your people just messed up. When should you pull them aside to have a corrective feedback conversation?

We often hear that we should provide immediate feedback. I'd like to just mention a word of caution here. In some cases, we may need to take some time to cool down a bit, to think it through, and to consider what consequences may be in order.

Sometimes, allowing yourself a few hours, or even a day or so, to contemplate the situation is wise. You may also want to get counsel from a peer or your boss before taking corrective action. Giving corrective feedback when you're angry or frustrated will not have the right tone or impact. So, you may want to consider giving it a little time. Don't take a month, but waiting a few hours or until the next day might be a good idea.

Improvement on an individual and team level only happens when we are in an environment where coaching is expected, mistakes are permitted, and corrective feedback conversations are frequent and effective.

DON'T SKIP THE POSITIVE

I realize that I'm focusing on difficult, constructive, and maybe even negative interactions here. I'm stressing *corrective* feedback, rather than reinforcing feedback, recognition, and praise in this short overview.

That's by design, as again I'm trying to tip the scales a bit. While many of us fail to provide enough positive feedback out of busyness or neglect, we tend to *actively* avoid providing the negative.

It's not the purpose of this chapter to convince you of the need for *positive* interactions. I'll just say that there's plenty of research supporting the importance of a positive environment. In fact, studies show that for a work environment to be considered *healthy*, positive interactions should outweigh negative ones by at least *five to one*. These are not just formal moments of recognition, feedback, or praise, but a general tenor of positive, friendly interactions throughout the day. We don't need formal "happy hours" to create a positive environment, just frequent happy *interactions*.

It should be obvious that a good leader is generous with his or her praise and gratitude for jobs well done. We should take the time to appreciate people, thank them, recognize great performance or improvement, and provide positive feedback. Just keep those moments separate from the corrective feedback meetings whenever possible.

Here's another thing to think about when giving positive feedback or praise: People are different when it comes to recognition.

Some are motivated by public recognition. Some prefer not to receive public recognition. It's important not to assume that your people enjoy exactly the same format of recognition that you do. So, ask them. Ask them if it's okay to recognize them in front of the team, or whether that will embarrass them. Ask each of your people what type of praise and recognition is most meaningful to them personally.

Then try to speak their praise language when they do good work.

To sum up, while frequent, specific, *positive* feedback is critically important to create a healthy and enjoyable work environment, the key to maximizing results is to address behaviors that need *improvement*.

PUTTING IT TOGETHER

When it comes to real-life leadership, we must take seriously our responsibility to provide corrective feedback when it's needed.

First, set the expectation that you will have a culture of coaching, and that corrective feedback should be expected for individual and group improvement.

Second, when it's time to provide corrective feedback, skip the sandwich and use the B.L.T. method. Be direct about what you need to talk about and why. Listen by admitting you may not have all the information and asking for their perspective on the issue. Then transition out of the meeting by getting a commitment and explaining any consequences that are necessary.

Finally, be sure that the overall environment is still one where positive feedback and interactions far outweigh negative ones, and praise and appreciation are doled out generously in public or in private as the individuals prefer.

Maximizing results requires a leader to have tough conversations often. When they're done right, with the right spirit, relationships are preserved, and performance improvement will happen.

THREE POINTS, FIVE QUESTIONS, AND ONE ACTION

Three Points to Review

- Most leaders feel a real fear about providing negative feedback and therefore tend to avoid it.

- We can create a culture of coaching that permits frequent constructive feedback while remaining characterized by positivity and friendly interactions.

- Having constructive feedback conversations are easier with a simple, honest, structured approach that allows for a smooth transition and maintained relationship.

Five Questions to Consider

1. Is there a general spirit of defensiveness and excuse-making on my team?

2. Do I spend enough time recognizing good performance and behavior?

3. Do I need to provide permission to my team to give me coaching about my leadership?

4. When I share criticism or correct an associate, do I get to the point, while communicating a spirit of openness?

5. Do my "coaching" sessions have dialogue?

One Action to Take

✓ At your next staff meeting or in one-on-ones, share your desire to create a coaching culture, provide permission to be coached on your leading, and ask for permission to share feedback more often.

10 GETTING CHANGE TO STICK

If you're trying to hit a fastball travelling at hundred miles per hour, three times out of ten is excellent. A baseball player with that average over time is likely a future hall-of-famer.

However, when it comes to the constantly changing demands of today's organizational environment, missing the ball seven out of ten times just won't cut it. But that's where we are. It's widely estimated that up to 70% of all change efforts fail to achieve their desired result. While that claim has proven hard to substantiate, I think we can all agree that many of the change efforts we've been a part of have been painful at best and utter failures at worst.

It seems to me that if we could use our roles as leaders to reverse that reality, we'd be hailed as heroes. Wouldn't it be great if we could help our teams progress more smoothly through the chaos of constant change?

Change researchers agree that *change* is not the problem in most cases. It's *resistance* to change that creates the issues.

In my work with personality theory, I've learned that

about half the population is naturally wired to prefer stability and the status quo. For many, change (even good change) is just uncomfortable. Furthermore, that same personality work has shown that employees below the management level are even more likely to have a preference for predictability and are therefore even more likely to resist change. So, right out of the gate, we have a difficult uphill climb just to gain acceptance for needed changes.

Change is going to happen. It can happen one of two ways. It can be *managed*, or it can be *unmanaged*. Unmanaged change is dangerous. In a sense, it's leaving things to chance. It's using hope as a strategy. Hope that the desired change will happen, stay in place, and be embraced by everyone involved.

WHAT IS "CHANGE MANAGEMENT"?

Let's break down the definition of change management by looking at both words. A *change* is the act of making or becoming different. *Management* is the process of dealing with or controlling things or people. Why do we "control" things? It's so they turn out the way we *want* them to.

If we put those two definitions together, we have this: *Change management is the process of controlling the act of making something different...so it turns out the way we want it to!*

As leaders of people, we have a responsibility to be involved in the changes required of us and our teams. Making sure changes stick is not HR's job. It's not a project manager's job. It's not the job of the senior leadership team. It's ours.

THE FIVE ROLES YOU PLAY IN CHANGE

There are five roles you play when it comes to change in your organization. Remembering these five roles can be difficult when in the heat of the battle, so it can help to use an acrostic. I use this memory-jogging sentence: "Change Strategy Gets Lasting Results." (CSGLR)

Communicator

"C" stands for the role of *Communicator*. When change is needed in an organization, managers are needed to assist with frequent, meaningful communication.

To get the attention of busy employees, managers must carry the clear message to them. It's too easy to tune out messages from HR or "corporate" at times. Those business partners need us as leaders to help get the information through.

We play the role of communicator by listening for the key messages from change implementers and reinforcing and repeating that information in our individual and group meetings. If someone asks us to "cascade" information to our teams, we make it a priority to do it.

Supporter

"S" stands for the role of *Supporter*. Employees must see visible support from their supervisors and managers when it comes to the change at hand.

We need to be very careful to avoid the temptation to commiserate or complain about the change with them. Even if we question things ourselves, we should never blame our bosses or contribute to the resistance felt among our employees.

I sometimes get pushback from managers on this point. They will often say that it feels dishonest to "put on a happy face" about a change that they don't like.

I totally get it. Most of us are not just leaders, but also followers subject to decisions and changes handed down from above. Many of us get to deal with our own issues caused by bosses that don't lead all that well themselves.

When we don't like a change and find it hard to support it, it's important to go up the chain or directly to the one rolling out the change to understand its rationale, purpose, and necessity. Even if we leave that conversation uninspired, it's important to demonstrate to our team that we will support the change and do our best to make it a success.

Guide

"G" is for the role of *Guide*. Imagine you've hired a guide to lead you through a tricky and dangerous mountain pass, but just as you get to the hardest part, he disappears, and you're on your own. This would be unnerving even if you had detailed knowledge about how to traverse the pass. Having the experienced guide there provides comfort and confidence that things will turn out okay.

This is what it feels like when we disappear or demonstrate disinterest in helping. We need to be available to our team as a guide when the change starts to happen. This means that we ourselves understand the change and stay present and willing to provide help or guidance during the transition.

Liaison

"L" is for the role of *Liaison*. When change is rolled out, supervisors need to be intermediaries between their people and the project team or department rolling out the change.

It's our job to relay information in *both* directions as needed. We need to especially relay rumors, questions, or concerns from our team members to those that can provide clarity, answer questions, and resolve concerns.

Researcher Brené Brown talks about change and the power of rumors. She says that when people don't have data, they fill the gaps with their own beliefs and fears to make the stories complete. In the absence of complete facts and clear information, rumors are born. Usually, they don't help.

Resistance Manager

Finally, the "R" stands for the role of *Resistance Manager*. As I shared earlier, it can be expected that half or more of our people may be resistant to change. Employee resistance is arguably the single largest reason that changes fail.

As leaders, we are the first line of defense for managing resistance to change. We're the ones most likely to hear the concerns and complaints. We can identify those who show signs of resistance and help them through their concerns most effectively.

Many years ago, a researcher named Elisabeth Kubler-Ross identified the stages of grief a person experiences after the loss of a loved one. She displayed those stages by graphing them in the form of a well-known curve starting with initial shock and denial and moving to final acceptance. See Figure 4.0 for a modified version of Kubler-Ross's famous grief curve.

Figure 4.0

Change researchers have found that there's a similar curve as a person experiences the loss of the *status quo* during change. In the middle of that curve is something we affectionately call the "valley of despair." It's a very normal phenomenon as people move through change. It's the low part of the curve where denial and anger turn to depression and discouragement.

While proactively managing change doesn't avoid the valley of despair, it usually helps to shorten its depth and duration.

I share this concept of a *grief curve* in the context of change because I think we can learn two key things from it.

First, change acceptance takes *time*. There's no way around it. People will move through the stages of grief at different paces and in different degrees. We should expect this to happen as those with a higher natural preference for stability react more strongly and resist longer.

Second, there are going to be *emotions* involved, and emotions can be uncomfortable. I love the correlation to Kubler-Ross's grief curve because of the parallels to our emotional reactions to loss. When we lose something we love, we grieve. Make no mistake, there are those among us who *love* the stable, comfortable, predictable work life that is lost (at least for a time) when change is thrust upon us.

As leaders who hope to assist in the change management process, it's important that we remember these issues of time and emotions so we're not surprised or frustrated by the challenges we face just trying to roll out a *simple* change.

CHANGE MANAGEMENT 101

Before ending this chapter on the leader's roles in getting change to stick, I want to provide a little practical help and exposure to change management as a discipline.

Many of you may be in an organization that lacks formal change management. Most leaders and managers in small and midsize organizations don't have the luxury of relying on internal or external change management consultants. In many cases, we don't even have formal *project* managers to help roll things out. If this is you, you may need to don the hat of change manager to some extent. I'd like to help you do just that, without turning this into a practitioner's textbook on change management.

Like a lot of disciplines, formal change management has yielded several excellent models and frameworks. I like a lot of them, but I also believe in general that *simpler is better*. Simple allows us to recall things, so we just might actually *use* them when we need them.

If this stuff intrigues you, you're certainly welcome to study other change management models, but I'd like to just briefly mention one that's been around since 1947.

It's Kurt Lewin's three stage model.

Lewin's Three Stage Model

Lewin's model is commonly referred to as the *Unfreeze, Change, Refreeze* model. In this simple way of looking at change, we find that there are actions we should take *before* we change something and *after* we change it.

In the *unfreeze* stage, we concentrate on creating and sharing the compelling reasons and rationale for the change, preparing and documenting all the information needed, planning a thorough communication and training strategy, and anticipating where we might expect resistance to occur.

During the *change*, we are obviously concentrating on frequent communication, ongoing dialogue, formal training, implementing the required policies, processes, and procedures, and testing to be sure the change is working properly. This is the part of change management that usually gets most of the focus.

After the bulk of the change is in place, the *refreeze* stage calls for us to ensure that people and processes don't snap back to the former way of doing things. We do this by formalizing and enforcing the new methods, structures, expectations, and processes to solidify the new way of doing things. During this third stage, we also should be staying alert to the need for continued training and support as the new reality starts to take shape.

I don't share this over-simplified summary of Lewin's model to imply that managing change is a predictable "color-by-numbers" activity. I share this so you begin to think about those pre- and post-activities and actions that need to accompany any successful change effort.

Again, this is certainly just a cursory overview of a change management discipline that deserves a lot more attention. I encourage you to become a student of change management, especially if you find yourself having to step up to that role in your current employment situation.

PUTTING IT TOGETHER

Let's summarize the main points about a leader's role in making change stick.

First, change is constant and inevitable. (We all know that.)

Second, resistance to change is normal. For many, resistance to change is hard-wired into their personalities. We should expect that there will be emotions involved as some on our team experience discomfort and grieve the loss of the way things used to be.

Third, supervisors and managers are uniquely positioned to play key roles in getting changes to stick. We are the communicators, supporters, guides, liaisons, and resistance managers of the change process.

Finally, remember our friend Kurt Lewin taught us that before we change something, we need to *unfreeze* it. (I'm not sure why he didn't say "thaw.") Then after the change is made, we need to do some *refreezing* to make sure things don't revert to their original form.

Remember, unmanaged change is *dangerous*. It's like a strategy of hope. Getting change to stick is *not* someone else's role. It's ours. Our people are watching us for our reaction to change, and they're looking to us for reassurance that everything will be okay on the other side.

THREE POINTS, FIVE QUESTIONS, AND ONE ACTION

Three Points to Review

- Change is going to happen, and we as leaders need to play an active role in getting it to stick.

- People are going to resist change because it's normal to do so, and we need to be prepared for it.

- Effective change requires that we prepare for the change and solidify it when it's done.

Five Questions to Consider

1. Do I take the time to read all communications about the changes being rolled out to my team?

2. Do I create dialogue with my team to ensure they understand the what, why, when, and how of changes?

3. Am I leading by example and attending training or meetings designed to explain the change?

4. When I don't like or understand a change, do I tend to commiserate or complain along with my team?

5. If I sense resistance on my team, am I confronting it so I can understand and help to resolve concerns proactively?

One Action to Take

✓ Go to your team this week and ask specifically what rumors are out there about an ongoing or impending change.

11 EMBRACING CONFLICT

It's Sunday night. Your mind turns to starting your workweek tomorrow morning. Suddenly, that feeling of dread starts in the pit of your stomach as you think of the conflict you're having with a coworker. Your pulse starts to race, and you can feel heat rising into your face at just the thought of sitting in another meeting with him.

I don't know if that rings true for you, but that feeling of dread, stress, and anxiety is a common occurrence for millions of people in organizations all over the world.

In the US, conflict costs employers hundreds of millions of dollars each year in productivity as employees and managers spend time every day dealing with conflict rather than their primary goals and objectives.[5]

To further compound the problem, there are the harder-to-quantify, conflict-driven, stress-related health and engagement costs, which easily add another billion

---

[5] *Workplace Conflict and How Businesses Can Harness It to Thrive*, CPP Global Human Capital Report, July 2008.

dollars in costs each year.

Is the answer to get rid of workplace conflict? That would be nice, but it's not going to happen, as long as we humans are still in the workplace.

Conflict is a normal human condition. It is *not* a sign of dysfunction or toxicity. Nor is it a reason to panic or quit. However, unbridled, pervasive, and unresolved conflict *absolutely* results in cultural damage that often can't be repaired. For many, many employees, this becomes a primary reason for quitting.

While we can't eliminate conflict from our experience, I think we *can* do two things.

First, we may be able to avoid *some* conflict, as we raise awareness, improve communication practices, and promote personal development.

Second, we need to accept that conflict is a normal human condition and work hard to embrace it, harness it, and get better at working through it together. It's this second approach that I'll address in this chapter. In addition, I'll share a few practical tips for you to use when you find yourself intervening in and mediating conflict on the team.

PUTTING THE OXYGEN MASK ON OURSELVES FIRST

The first thing to realize as leaders is that we are *not* immune to conflict ourselves. We have plenty of opportunity for conflict with our peers, our boss, our staff, and even our clients. We are just as prone to interpersonal conflict and anger as anyone else. In fact, we may even be more prone to conflict since many of us have strong, action-oriented, and sometimes dominant personalities.

So, when it comes to conflict, we're going to follow the flight attendant's advice and put the oxygen mask on ourselves *before* assisting our teams.

To do this, I want start by briefly explaining what happens to us physiologically during conflict.

Sometimes we're tempted to think that we should just be able to "control" ourselves and not get pulled into heated conflict. We think we should be able to just stay calm and think our way through a disagreement. However, conflict doesn't work that way. We're actually dealing with a physiological reaction coming from deep within our brains.

When we perceive a threat, our amygdala sounds an alarm. Our hypothalamus then activates the sympathetic nervous system, releasing a flood of stress hormones like adrenaline and cortisol into our system. This prepares us for "fight or flight." When this deeply instinctive function takes over, we call it being "triggered."

We notice immediate changes in our bodies. We experience an increased heart rate, shallow breathing, sweaty palms, a dry mouth, and sometimes even a tunnel-like vision as our body prepares for action. The active amygdala also shuts down the neural pathways to our prefrontal cortex. When that happens, we can become disoriented, lose our complex decision-making and communication abilities, and become blinded to other perspectives beyond our own.

When we're in this flooded state, we can't choose how

we want to react because our hard-wired nervous system does it for us. There is no communicating or reasoning our way out of it. All we can really do once triggered is wait until our autonomic nervous system is back in balance. When we find ourselves in this flooded state, it's a great idea to request a break for a bit. Before saying something we'll later regret, it might be best to say something like, "I'm kind of upset right now. I need a little time to process things before we continue." So, take a break. Find a quiet place or go for a walk.

Research shows that once our sympathetic nervous system has been activated, it takes at least 20-30 minutes for our heart rate to normalize and our system to be back in balance. When you take the break, avoid venting, fuming, or reviewing your argument. Instead, breathe deeply and think about happier things.

Breathe and Think Happy Thoughts

I won't attempt to explain why deep breathing restores balance to our nervous system and brings our cognitive abilities back online, but it does. In fact, the Navy Seals use something called Box Breathing to recover from real-life fight or flight situations. (See Figure 5.0) It involves inhaling for a slow count of four, holding your breath for a count of four, exhaling for a count of four, and again holding your breath for a count of four before inhaling again. I guess if it's good enough for the Navy Seals, it's good enough for our challenges with that one guy who seems to push all our buttons.

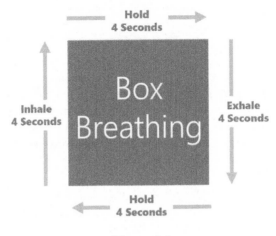

Figure 5.0

So, do your box breathing for five or ten minutes, thinking only of your slow breathing and your favorite secluded beach or other relaxing place. It's also helpful, after several cycles of box breathing, to ask yourself some questions like, "What emotion am I feeling?" "What caused me to feel that way?" "What do I want that I'm not getting?"

Once you've taken your break and brought your pre-frontal cortex back online, you're ready to resume the conversation. I recommend you come back to the conversation and do the following:

First, thank them for allowing you to take some time. Showing appreciation for their patience is not just courteous, it also shows humility and can be disarming as you begin the difficult conversation again.

Second, use an "I" statement and explain the emotion you were feeling. Try not to use the word "angry" if possible. Instead think about more specific emotions like feeling unfairly treated, unheard, disappointed, hurt, or disrespected.

Third, it's helpful to reset things by returning to a shared objective and agreeing that you both want what's best for the team, department, organization, or customer. Sometimes a simple change in perspective back to the organization's mission or customer needs will depersonalize the issue and bring two combatants back to the same side of the table.

So that's what happens in our bodies when we get into heated conflict, and a couple ways to cope with it. If nothing else, I hope it has sparked an interest in understanding your own personal physiology, triggers, and reactions. I recommend further study on topics like emotional intelligence, stress management, and personality theory to continue to grow in self-awareness.

HOW TO DEAL WITH CONFLICT ON THE TEAM

Now it's time to turn our attention to how you as leader can help your team deal with conflict. Ultimately, we want to develop our people so they can navigate through conflict on their own. But that takes time and is dependent on people being willing to learn.

While our goal should be to grow our team's conflict and interpersonal skills, we need to be prepared to intervene and assist in resolving conflicts happening right now. Remember, unresolved, festering, and repeated conflict leads to dysfunction, cultural toxicity, and usually unwanted turnover of good employees. It's because of this that we need to step in and do something when it surfaces.

Six Tips for Mediating Conflicts

There are mountains of great books and articles filled with conflict mediation ideas and strategies. It's not my purpose here to address conflict resolution in detail. It's a discipline worthy of its own in-depth study. However, assuming you don't have immediate plans to enroll in a formal conflict management course, here are my six quick tips for helping your team members work through conflict.

First, meet with the people in conflict together as soon as possible. It's tempting, and feels more comfortable, to separate the combatants and only meet with them individually. Don't do it. If you allow each to tell his or her "side of the story" in private, it becomes their only goal to convince you, whom they see as the judge and jury, of the merits of their case. The goals of perspective, compromise, and resolution are lost as they strive only to highlight their position and denigrate all the others to win your favor and support.

Sometimes, briefly meeting alone with a person in conflict may be necessary as you first become aware of an issue needing resolution. It may even be helpful to let someone vent to you for a bit. But as soon as you sense there's a conflict going on involving someone else, you need to press pause and arrange for a meeting with everyone involved.

Second, when you have a conflict resolution meeting, start by describing the plan for the conversation and get acknowledgment from both parties on the rules. You might say something like, "I understand you two are experiencing some conflict. Here's how I'd like to handle this meeting."

After explaining your plan and the ground rules, ask if it sounds okay to everyone before moving forward. This helps set the table for a more calm, respectful, and systematic discussion.

Third, give each person in conflict the opportunity to briefly share his or her point of view, uninterrupted by the other person. You, however, should feel free to interject short clarifying questions along the way so you're able to understand what's being shared.

After both have had a chance to share, ask each person if they'd like clarification on anything said by the other person. Remember to step in and immediately coach or enforce the ground rules you established if things start to get out of hand.

Fourth, depersonalize the disagreement. A key strategy to keep people from slipping into fight or flight mode is to depersonalize the conflict. One way to do this is to remove the shame associated with conflict and explain that it's completely normal, it's expected, and it happens to all of us. I like to share that our different personalities cause us to bump heads as our internal priorities, tendencies, and natural desires conflict with others. This is also a great time for you to share your confidence that both are reasonable, intelligent, well-meaning people. Tell them that conflict is usually a sign of passionate people and that you'd rather have passionate people than not.

As I mentioned earlier, you can also confirm that you all just need to focus on what's best for the organization and its customers. This appeal to a shared vision can sometimes shed light on a self-focused agenda, leading to compromise and reconciliation.

Fifth, when in doubt, ask questions. As a mediator of conflict, questions are your best friend. Someone once said, "Knowledge is having the right answer. Wisdom is asking the right questions."

In my office, I have a large wooden question mark hanging on a nail on the wall because I need the visual reminder to shut up and ask more questions. It doesn't always work, but when I see it, I do tend to pause and demonstrate more curiosity.

When we ask questions in conflict meetings, we move people off their rehearsed testimony and list of accusations, and direct them to deeper thinking, contemplation, and solution finding. Asking questions like, "Mary, what do you need more of or less of from Tom in order to feel better about this?" Or "Tom, what can you now appreciate about Mary's point of view on this issue?"

I also love to use a variation of the *start-stop-continue* technique and ask each to describe what they'd like to see the other start doing or stop doing to resolve the disagreement.

My final tip for mediating conflict is to call for a break if you sense that one or both people have been triggered and are experiencing the symptoms of an activated sympathetic nervous system. Once this has happened, effective communication, complex problem solving, memory recall, and the ability to see other perspectives is impossible. The body is flooded with stress hormones, and those things just don't have priority access to our brain. To make matters worse, when sitting in a room with the "enemy," unable to freeze or flee, *fight* feels like the only option.

When you recognize this, call for a 30-minute break to give time for emotions to normalize. Then reconvene, readdress the ground rules, and start asking thoughtful questions again.

SEEING CONFLICT DIFFERENTLY

Let me just wrap up this brief overview by challenging you to see conflict differently. It's normal. It's a sign of passionate people. It can be harnessed and embraced to promote teamwork and better decisions.

However, if your team is like nearly every other team, you *will* need to intervene to help resolve disputes and conflicts. Perhaps over time, you'll be able to guide your team to develop the mindset and skillset to interact more peaceably together and self-resolve conflict when it arises, without your direct involvement. Until then, we need to lead in this area.

Remember, it starts with you recognizing your own physiological reaction to conflict and developing your ability to self-soothe and restore balance to your nervous system. As your team sees this in you, they'll have a built-in role model for growth as they develop their own ability to cope with this natural, universal human condition.

THREE POINTS, FIVE QUESTIONS, AND ONE ACTION

Three Points to Review

- Conflict is normal and can't be avoided altogether, but it can be embraced and harnessed to drive better teamwork, problem solving, and decision making.

- As leaders, we need to first recognize our own physiological reactions while in conflict and learn to maintain strong working relationships.

- Our teams will need us to actively engage in conflict mediation as they develop the ability to self-resolve conflicts among themselves.

Five Questions to Consider

1. When I start to get "triggered," what physical reactions do I feel?

2. Have I set the expectation for my team that when we disagree, we'll work it out together?

3. Do I get frustrated when conflict happens on my team?

4. Are hurt feelings and offenses addressed quickly when they happen, or do I allow them to burn out of control?

5. Do I see conflict as a good thing because it can bring issues to the surface that can make us better?

One Action to Take

✓ Go to the individuals on your team and directly ask if there are any unresolved conflicts simmering below the surface of the team. Probe for conflicts between your team and other teams as well.

12 DEVELOPING PEOPLE

Imagine with me that it's a thousand years ago. You own a large flock of sheep, and that flock is the primary source of income for you and your family. You've carefully chosen a good shepherd to be a steward over this most valuable possession.

What objectives do you give him? What is his true measure of success as the shepherd of your flock? It's the growth and development of each and every sheep. Success is not just keeping the sheep alive until market time. Success is measured by how big and healthy those sheep become. Did they grow and develop thick and healthy wool coats for shearing? Did they eat well and get enough rest to add body weight so that they generate the best price at market? The impact of a shepherd is best measured by the growth and development of the sheep.

In our organizations, helping our people grow is the ultimate in "others focus." When we commit to developing the people under our care, we demonstrate the true heart of a shepherd-style leader. Every minute we spend helping someone grow is a minute we aren't focused on our own selfish ambitions.

Studies continue to show that the availability of growth opportunities is a top driver of employee satisfaction and loyalty. One comprehensive study showed that lack of career growth was a top reason employees leave a company and that growth *potential* is a top reason that millennials would consider switching companies.[6] Gallup adds to this mounting evidence, saying that 87% of millennials indicate that development is important in a job.[7]

The younger generations are demanding growth and development. This is a huge issue because in 2016, millennials became the largest generation in the labor force. In fact, we started to see the generation after the millennials enter the workforce in 2018, and they're showing an even greater appetite for growth. So, it's imperative that we do our part to develop and grow our people.

Author and leadership expert Ken Blanchard has said that the true goal of any teacher should be for all students to get an "A." Not all will work hard enough to get one, so it may not happen, but the teacher's goal is unchanged.

Imagine if a teacher stood in front of his or her class and said, "My goal is for about 15% of you to get A's, about 15% of you to flunk this class, and the rest of you to just get somewhere between a B and a D."

That would be ridiculous. The goal should be that

---

[6] *INFOGRAPHIC: The Age of Social Recruiting*, by Glassdoor Team, 2013.
[7] *Millennials Want Jobs to Be Development Opportunities,* by Amy Adkins and Brandon Rigoni, Gallup Workplace, 2016.

every single one of our people grows where they need to grow so they can all be "A players."

I spent most of my career as a leader viewing the development plans of my people as an after-thought of the performance plan. It was just something HR required on the last page of the appraisal document. I would just try to identify a training class or two so I could check a box. Not much time was spent carefully assessing needs and selecting development areas for myself or my people. My focus was on performance, not development.

Let me be clear: an effective focus on growth is not handing someone a training catalog and saying, "Pick a couple." It should be a more central point of discussion, carrying the weight and importance approaching that of performance objectives themselves.

THE THREE "P's" OF DEVELOPMENT

To become leaders with a fundamental focus on developing people, we need to recognize specific needs for development. I like to evaluate development needs in three categories to ensure the correct growth areas are targeted. There are times when specific development needs may take precedence over others.

Some have development needs in the area of *performance*. When an employee is falling short in a key area of job performance, this becomes the first priority for development. An employee failing to meet expectations in one or more essential job duties is in career jeopardy. This is not the time to send them to get additional certifications or other forms of development. It's better to spend available development time and budget on helping them grow skills or experience in the requirements of their current role.

The second area of focus is *professional* development. This is helping an employee with career advancement through the gaining of new technical or professional capabilities. These might be include pursuing an advanced degree, studying for a new certification, attending seminars, participating in job rotation, or being assigned to temporary projects.

The third growth category is that of *personal* development. This third category complements the first two by allowing us to look at the soft skill needs of each employee. We all have opportunities for improvement in our relationships, communication, coping with conflict, self-awareness, or emotional intelligence. It's important when creating development plans to address any interpersonal challenges or deficiencies that might be holding the employee back. To make this easier, each year you might consider a team-wide focus on a particular topic, in order to grow together as team.

In short, we need to match up growth opportunities and expectations to each person based on where they are and where they need or want to go, using the three development areas of performance, professional, and personal.

EMPLOYEE OWNERSHIP OF DEVELOPMENT

Individual development plans need to be owned by the *individual*. Each person must buy into it and be committed to his or her own personal growth. Keep in mind, however, that development appetite comes in degrees. Not everyone on your team will have the same desire for growth and development. Some are content professionally and aren't seeking a lot of stretch assignments. It's best to match up highly growth-focused people with aggressive development opportunities, and the less growth-focused with less aggressive tactics. If a person has little or no interest in development, you probably just need to address any skill gaps impacting daily performance. In these cases, there's no need to create an aggressive, detailed, multi-phasic training plan, but still, make sure all are involved in growth to some degree.

Growth plans don't need to be exhaustive or complicated. Sometimes, a singular focus is appropriate as you seek to facilitate real and lasting growth in one particular area.

GROWTH CAN'T BE FORCED

If growth is going to happen, it needs to happen naturally. Intrinsically. It must come from within each person on your team. In other words, it can't be forced.

Our job as leaders is to create an environment conducive to growth. We need to do what we can to foster, encourage, and enable growth to happen.

Imagine you want to plant a new tree in your yard. What do you do? You carefully choose the right location for the tree. You determine whether it will get the sunlight and water required by that unique variety of tree. Then, you dig the right size hole to accommodate the root ball. You prepare the soil in the hole and maybe even sprinkle on some root starter fertilizer. After planting, you diligently water the young tree, encouraging it to grow with fertile, moist, nutrient-rich surroundings. Essentially, you do everything you can to set the tree up for success.

But then, it's up to the tree.

Here's what you don't do: you don't grab the trunk with both hands and pull upwards to force the tree to get taller faster.

The growth happens from within the tree.

Leadership and management expert Dan Rockwell once said, "Trying to fix someone is insulting to them and arrogant of you. Development is a partnership, not a dictatorship."

CREATING AN ENVIRONMENT FOR GROWTH

There are four essential ways that we as leaders can create an environment conducive to growth.

First, we do this by modeling a growth mindset ourselves. It's important that our people see us seeking personal growth, professional growth, and growth in our commitment to perform well as leaders. We need to recognize and share with others our own need for improvement.

We need to understand that it's okay to have gaps and struggles and deficiencies, even as leaders. It makes us human. We can take personality assessments, utilize 360-degree feedback reviews, and pursue other ways to demonstrate an openness to growth and learning. Hiding, masking, or denying our own imperfection doesn't help.

Second, we need to destroy the *myth of perfectionism* in the workplace. Some organizations stress results and performance so intensely that errors and imperfection carry a powerful stigma. This often leads to pronounced anxiety and extreme defensiveness as people try to avoid even a hint of failure or blame.

If this is part of our culture, we need to communicate that nobody is expected to be *perfect*. Instead, everyone is expected to be *growing*. Including you. Nobody's performance is perfect. Nobody's skills, attitudes, relationships, work ethic, and professional knowledge are perfect and complete. We destroy the myth of perfectionism when we communicate that we all have room to grow, and it's okay.

Third, we shift weight from a heavy focus on performance with a little growth to a more balanced equation. As I admitted earlier, when I managed people, my focus was overwhelmingly on performance with a little token focus on development thrown in. A development-minded leader will have more balance and reward growth and improvement alongside solid results and performance.

Fourth, we need to provide the structure to shape the growth. There's a saying among several legendary football coaches—and stolen by my own high school coach—that says, "You either get better or you get worse, but you never stay the same."

The second law of thermodynamics is a law of physics stating that entropy (which is the opposite of growth) increases over time. That law applies to a closed system, which means if there is no connection to the outside, things wind down and get worse, not better.

Growth only happens when two elements are introduced: *energy* and *structure*.

The *energy* required for growth includes the things we've been talking about so far: your example, your encouragement, and your commitment to helping your people see themselves clearly and grow both personally and professionally.

The *structure* is the set of opportunities and mechanisms provided for growth. It's also setting aside budget and time to allow growth to happen. It's making available the opportunities that will shape growth in the direction best for the person, your team, and the organization.

Think of those opportunities as lattice for a plant. Lattice creates a path and shape for growth. Without lattice or structure, growth isn't directed in any particularly helpful direction, it just follows the path of least resistance.

Even when budgets are tight for outside training, there are ways to promote growth and continuous learning. We may have to get creative, but there are many inexpensive and even free ways to promote development and growth. Here are several to get your creative juices flowing: You could assign a "research" project with a team readout at the end. You could host (or assign leadership) for a book club that examines important topics. You could arrange for job shadowing or temporary work assignments to create exposure to new departments. You could invest some of your time to mentor younger associates. Be creative and gather ideas from those you lead.

Lastly, I'd like to share just one technique you might consider in the formation of personalized development plans for your people.

BE SOCRATIC

Dr. Mark Lepper, professor of psychology at Stanford, recommends a Socratic coaching approach. When you hear the word "Socratic," just think *questions*. Use open-ended questions to identify areas of needed growth and ask even more questions to generate possible solutions.

Rather than "prescribing" a set of training courses or mandating a development area, it's better to ask questions to allow people to self-identify needs for improvement. For instance, ask a question like, *"When you're doing your job, is there anything that causes you stress, or anywhere you feel less confident?"* Asking questions allows the individual to offer up options for development. If they don't match what you believe should be the focus, be patient and keep the dialogue flowing. If, after trying, the individual just doesn't see the same need for improvement that you do, try this question: *"If there was some issue or performance concern that was holding you back from maximum success, would you want me to tell you about it?"* This invites your feedback as the supervisor and has an air of concern for the well-being of the individual.

Outstanding tutors, coaches, and mentors use these questioning and dialogue techniques to create ownership in the growth plan. Obviously, just as a patient needing physical therapy can't be forced to do the exercises needed to heal, we know that the individual must buy into the plan and *want* to complete it.

PUTTNG IT TOGETHER

A leader's role as developer of people is fundamental. It's really the single greatest measure of success for a steward-oriented leader.

Further, we recognize that growth opportunities have become a primary employment expectation for employees. This is even more pronounced for the largest segment of our workforce and new entrants looking for jobs today.

Creating development plans takes a commitment to match up the specific needs, desires, and growth appetite of each individual. Not all people are hungry to learn and grow. It's not a good idea to force an aggressive development template onto everyone. However, be sure that even those who appear to be "comfortable" in their roles and uninterested in stretching skill levels are challenged to grow in a personal area or learn something new each year.

When we consider development areas for selection, we also must take care not to default to new technical or professional skills. Sometimes, shoring up a performance area or addressing a personal, character-building, soft skill may be much more impactful. For many, it's character, relationship, and emotional competencies that need the most attention.

Since we can't force growth to happen, we as leaders need to focus on creating an environment conducive to growth.

We model a growth and learning mindset ourselves by being open about our limitations and our commitment to growing as leaders and workers.

We destroy the myth of perfectionism, making imperfection okay and *growth,* not perfection, the expectation.

We rebalance our focus and expectations to value growth and continuous improvement as much as we value raw performance results.

We provide the structure, or "lattice," of growth opportunities to shape the growth toward effective and needed development areas.

Finally, remember the Socratic method. As we embark on a new commitment to ensure our people are being developed, consider adopting the coaching and tutoring strategy of some of the world's best teachers and *ask questions* when working on development plans with your people.

When leaders spend time considering the growth needs of their people and providing development opportunities, they are being the best versions of themselves. Promoting growth in others means that, at least for a time, we are not focused on our own ambitions and aspirations. Pride yourself on leaving a legacy of healthy, thriving, growing individuals. It truly is your finest measure of success.

THREE POINTS, FIVE QUESTIONS, AND ONE ACTION

Three Points to Review

- If you're not actively looking for ways to promote growth, development, and even "healing" in your people, you are not leading as a steward or good shepherd might.

- All people need at least *some* focus on growth to avoid stagnation, but not all people need or want an *aggressive* plan.

- We don't need a huge training budget to be developers of people, just creativity.

Five Questions to Consider

1. Do I have a plan for my own personal development?

2. Have I modeled a growth mindset by sharing with my team the things I'm working on as a leader, professional, or person?

3. Am I going to leave my people better off than when I found them?

4. Am I focused more on my next job, next team, next opportunity than I am on the people under my care right now?

5. Do I take my role as a steward of my organization's valuable resources seriously?

One Action to Take

✓ Make it a priority to have a one-on-one conversation with each of your team members and ask this question: "If you could learn one new thing, personally or professionally, this coming year, what would it be?"

13 INTEGRATED LEADERSHIP

My father and his wife live in Tennessee. Their home is surrounded by beautiful, well-constructed, and safe hiking trails. Every time we visit, we hike.

Often as we hike, we'll come upon a small bridge spanning a little creek or stream. They're made of treated lumber, they have carefully sanded handrails, and they are very sturdy. I'm a pretty big guy and those little bridges are more than up to the task. They have the structural integrity to handle frequent foot traffic for decades. However, I wouldn't want to drive a bulldozer over it. For that you'd need a much stronger bridge with a different *make-up*. You'd need a bridge made with steel and concrete to withstand the demands of that purpose. In fact, those little footbridges in Tennessee were built by a Trails Committee, on which was a retired structural engineer who had designed bridges for a living. He knew what was needed for that bridge to do its job!

Author Dr. Henry Cloud in his book *Integrity: The Courage to Meet the Demands of Reality* describes the integrity needed to be a highly successful leader. I owe a debt of gratitude to Dr. Cloud for opening my eyes to a new definition of integrity. Much of what I call "integrated leadership" comes from the insights received from reading his work on this subject.

WHAT IS INTEGRITY?

What distinguishes an active, aware leader from everyone else? Why is it that some people seem to be more capable of motivating, coaching, encouraging, challenging, protecting, developing, and truly leading others?

Further, why is it that people can attend the same leadership training courses, read the same books, hear the same instruction, and get the same encouragement, but remain unchanged? Why do people who possess the intelligence, training, and talent needed to be successful still fail to achieve everything they're capable of achieving? This has been a mystery since the first book on leadership or management was written.

Success in life, as a person, as an employee, or as a leader, is not just about what we know and what we can do. It's about who we *are*.

What do you think of when you hear the word "integrity"? If you're like most, you may think of integrity as a synonym for "honesty" or "character." Maybe you think about morals or ethics.

However, the word integrity has its root in the Latin word *integer*. Integer means whole or complete. An integer in arithmetic is a whole number as opposed to a fraction. So, integrity really speaks to a wholeness or soundness. According to Henry Cloud, having integrity is having a make-up that can stand up to the demands of reality.

As in our earlier bridge example, it's more like the way engineers use the word to describe *structural* integrity. Engineers ensure that an object has the structural integrity to handle the task for which it is being designed. If we are building a bridge, the make-up of the bridge (its materials, design, etc.) must stand up to the intended use.

If you think about it, the word integrity really should be used as an adjective rather than a noun. Integrity should be used to *describe* someone's character or make-up. Everyone has character of some sort. Not everyone has character *integrity*.

INTEGRATION

Integrate also comes from that same Latin root word *integer*. Simply put, to integrate is to combine parts into a whole. *Integration* is the process of becoming more complete or whole. It's a journey of development. Nobody starts their professional or leadership experience fully integrated. Said another way, leaders are not born, they're *built*.

Integration in our context here is the process of becoming more complete or whole as a leader. It's developing a make-up that *integrates* different priorities, behaviors, and ways of thinking so that we become balanced, complete, and able to stand up under the demands of leadership. It's about joining what we do with how we do it. It's being willing and able to focus on tasks without sacrificing a team mentality. It's integrating a focus on our own needs and desires with a focus on others.

If a person is an individual contributor expected to crunch budget numbers, or document lab results, or make milkshakes all day, they can be successful with a lower degree of character integrity. This is because *less* is expected of them.

However, if that person manages others, more is expected. Just as a bridge built to hold heavy vehicles is designed to meet the demands of that reality, leaders of others need the structural integrity to meet the demands of leadership.

Leading others well requires character integrity. It requires *integrated leadership*. It requires a far different make-up from an individual contributor. It requires that we pursue and develop the parts of our make-up or character that are lacking. (And we all have them.) We all have "flat sides" to our leadership character. We all have room to grow. It's adopting a mindset of humility and a focus on growth as we work to develop skills and commitment to do the things required of leaders. So, what is the *evidence* of active leadership? What are the things on a true leader's to-do list?

WHAT DO INTEGRATED LEADERS DO?

The short answer to this question comes from the title of this book: Leaders *Lead*. They lead. They *do* things. They get up every day and think, "What do my people need from me today?" Then, they *do* them.

This short book does not claim to be an exhaustive treatise on leadership, or even a full list of the observable, measurable tasks that leaders do as they lead. However, it does contain a very solid list of important things that demonstrate the omni-dimensional, well-rounded behaviors of an integrated leader that really leads. By way of review, here's that list in a nutshell:

- ***We stretch.*** It all starts with acknowledging and admitting the truth about our own leadership comfort zone and being willing to become omni-dimensional, well-rounded leaders who commit to stretching into behaviors that don't feel natural for us.

- ***We own time.*** We foundationally recognize that we'll do literally nothing as a leader until we first take ownership of our time by learning to focus, prioritize, and guard our available time in order to create margin in our days for leading.

- ***We understand people.*** We get to know our people as individuals by understanding as much as we can about their histories, their shaping influences, their personality types, and their personal readiness levels to take on the duties we expect of them. Showing this level of individual interest demonstrates our devotion to them and creates trust.

- ***We protect and respect.*** We act as protectors of our people by modeling respectful and honorable behavior, and then intervening if anyone is subjected to mistreatment like discrimination, harassment, bullying, teasing, belittling, etc. This takes compassion and courage.

- ***We chart the course.*** We plan and communicate a vision about where we're going as a team, our key strategies and priorities to get us there, and the goals and metrics to ensure we stay on course. This creates trust and reduces anxiety when things get confusing for the people on our teams.

- ***We select the best people.*** We see every person on our team as an important link in a chain and take seriously every opportunity we get to select new people. We work to pick good humans by assessing intangibles rather than just resume accomplishments.

- ***We get stuff done.*** We get the right things done right through our people by empowering and challenging them through effective, purposeful delegation without micromanagement.

- ***We maximize results.*** We get over our fear and start giving constructive feedback honestly and humbly to drive higher levels of achievement and results. We do this without sacrificing our efforts to create a positive work environment where positive interactions far outweigh negative ones.

- ***We get change to stick.*** We are actively involved in helping to make changes stick in our organizations by playing our key roles so our team can move through the normal stages of grief and begin to accept and integrate new realities.

- ***We embrace conflict.*** We become much more aware and accepting of conflict among team members, understand the physiological signs of it, and intervene when necessary to help people return to a state of team cohesiveness and camaraderie.

- ***We develop people.*** We work very hard to ensure

our people continue to grow personally, professionally, and performance-wise, so they stay vibrant and on track to reach their full potential. Developing people is what differentiates steward leaders from "hired hand" leaders.

WE ALL LEAVE A WAKE

One of my fondest childhood memories is spending time at my grandparents' cottage on a beautiful lake in Allegan County in southwest Michigan. My summers were filled with swimming, water skiing, fishing, and boating.

My grandfather had this awesome mint green 16-foot speedboat with a mammoth outboard motor that my dad always had to repair before we could use it. I remember riding in that boat, looking over the stern and watching the giant, undulating wake that motor would create as the boat moved through the water. It was mesmerizing. It was beautiful, balanced, continuous, and utterly inevitable.

In *Integrity*, Dr. Henry Cloud explains that as we move through life, we *all* leave a wake behind us. He describes one side of the wake as our accomplishments, achievements, and results, and the other side as our relationships, friendships, and the people with whom we have contact and impact.

When our character is integrated, we leave a nice balanced wake behind us. Both sides are fully developed, and there's a nice symmetry as we look back.

However, many of us don't have that balance. Often, one side is far more pronounced than the other. For some, the results side is impressive. It's filled with accomplishments, degrees, career achievements, and exceeded performance objectives. However, the relationship side is flat and underdeveloped. It's filled with broken friendships, failed marriages, and unhappy employees. For others, the relationship side of the wake is full and beautiful. It's teeming with close friendships, strong marriages, and devoted employees. But the results side is weak, with a failure to push through obstacles, overcome failure, or reach business goals.

Strong leaders, and effective people in general, consider and contemplate the wake they're leaving as they move through life. They seek to *integrate* both sides to achieve a balance.

YOUR LEADERSHIP LEGACY

We will all leave a legacy. It's up to each of us to decide what we want that to be. What will people say about us when we're gone?

Journalist David Brooks says that when we die, we'll be known for two types of values. He calls one type our "resume values." In our wake example, these are the results and accomplishments of our life. It's what we've done for *ourselves*. He calls the other type "eulogy values." They're our values as demonstrated by our character, our relationships, and what we've done for *others*.

If you think about it, it's the relationship side that most of us want discussed during our eulogies. We'd want the eulogist to speak of our attributes, our character, how much we were loved by others, and how much we loved them. In this context, a recitation of our degrees, certifications, job titles, and achievements seems a bit out of place and, well, meaningless.

As leaders, we will also have a *leadership eulogy* read when we leave. How will your people describe you when you (or they) move on to a new job? If the answer to that question at this moment makes you cringe, it's okay. It's not too late. It's never too late to admit mistakes and start to practice the skills of integrating results and relationships.

WHAT WILL YOU DO NOW?

In the early 1880s, a researcher named Hermann Ebbinghaus conducted a now-famous study on human memory. It was admittedly a limited study conducted on just one person: himself. He published his hypothesis in 1885 as *Über das Gedächtnis*. (Memory: A Contribution to Experimental Psychology).

In the study, Ebbinghaus memorized content and then repeatedly tested himself after various time periods, recording the results. He plotted his results on a graph creating what is now known as the "forgetting curve." His findings showed that we are very likely to lose a significant percentage of new knowledge obtained over a very short period of time. (See Figure 6.0)

In case you're tempted to dismiss Dr. Ebbinghaus' 1885 findings along with the bloodletting and leach treatments of early scientific yesteryear, I'll just mention that a 2015 study was able to replicate the forgetting curve findings with very similar results![9] So, stay with me.

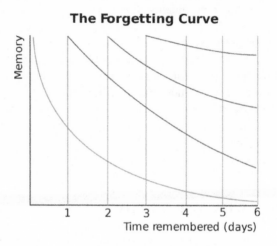

The Forgetting Curve

Figure 6.0

Ebbinghaus' study revealed that the moment we obtain new insights or information, we are at 100% knowledge retention. However, without reinforcement through repeated exposure or practical use, we'll lose 50% of that new knowledge after just one hour! We'll lose 70% after just one day. After six days, we'll have lost 90% of the new information or insight we gained.

That means that if you put this book down and do nothing to revisit these concepts from time to time, or fail to implement new leadership habits, you'll forget nearly *all* of what you have just learned. In fact, if this forgetting curve is even partially accurate, as of right now you have already forgotten most of what you read in the first ten chapters. That's a little depressing for any author, speaker,

---

[9] *Replication and Analysis of Ebbinghaus' Forgetting Curve*, Jaap M. J. Murre and Joeri Dros, 2015.

or trainer.

The good news also revealed by Ebbinghaus' study was that when we "recharge" our new knowledge by reviewing a concept, or taking an action, we briefly boost our knowledge retention back up to 100%. After each recharge event, our forgetting curve becomes a little flatter, and we retain more of the information for longer periods of time.

This means that we can actually create new neuropathways in our brains that play out in how we lead in our daily lives.

In short, do something.

Do the things of leadership every day. Assess your schedule every week to be sure you're stretching out of your comfort zone. Keep reviewing the recommendations in this book. Make a point to spend a little time each week recharging your knowledge about the things leaders to do really lead. Review often the *Three Points, Five Questions, and One Action* at the end of each chapter. Start using a leadership "Field Journal" to record your ideas, self-assessments, and insights about real-life leadership. Keep integrating your character by practicing the many varied skills and behaviors of a well-rounded leader.

Most importantly, be vulnerable with your team. Tell them you're committed to growing as a leader and that you know you have a long way to go. Ask them to be open about how you're doing.

Your people don't want a leader who thinks he or she has it all figured out. They know that's not true. They don't want a pretender. They want an authentic, approachable, vulnerable leader with an integrated character. They want to be able to relax knowing that you are committed to being both competent and caring.

Now, stop reading and go *lead.*

ABOUT THE AUTHOR

Jeff DeWolf is the founder of Wolf Prairie LLC, an organizational effectiveness and leadership development consultancy in Kansas City.

After researching the best studies of engagement and culture, Jeff created the JobHapp365™ assessment, which measures six critical workplace factors. Having witnessed the undeniable connection between cultural health and leadership quality, Jeff created the Real-Life Leadership™ program for equipping leaders at all levels to really lead.

Jeff loves to speak truth to leaders about their personal impact and the need to be omni-dimensional, "shepherd-style" leaders. He is also an Authorized Partner and Certified Facilitator for Everything DiSC® personality assessments and loves to use them for team building, personal development, and leadership coaching.

Jeff holds a bachelor's degree in Business Administration from the University of Michigan and a master's degree in Organization Development from Bowling Green State University.

Real-Life **Leadership**™

Wolf Prairie's Real-Life Leadership™ program is a set of interactive modules that incorporate the teachings of this book. Supervisors, managers, and leaders at all levels have benefitted from this training since 2017. Please visit wolfprairie.com for more information about this customizable, neuroscience-based, real-life leadership development opportunity.

Real-Life Learning™

wolfprairie.com

Made in the USA
Monee, IL
22 January 2022

88771298R00100